Jean-François Mallet

RECIPES FROM THE WOODS

The Book of Game and Forage

FOREWORD

—

I have always thought that it was as easy to cook a fillet of venison as a fillet or tenderloin of beef, as simple to roast a pheasant as a chicken, and as easy to make a wild boar stew as a *blanquette de veau*. All that's required is to just do it.

Above all, I want to demonstrate that cooking game frees us from what we have come to accept as the norm: stews that are too fatty, dishes that require interminable cooking and routine marinating that hides the true taste of lean and flavoursome meat. These can be replaced with lighter sauces, unexpected combinations of ingredients and simpler cooking methods. However, originality need not exclude tradition as long as it is revisited.

Whether people like to hunt or they simply enjoy going for a walk in the woods, they can take the opportunity to gather mushrooms or chestnuts and pick blackberries, blueberries or wild strawberries. As well as inspiring you to cook game, I want you to discover simple, original recipes for making the most of the wild foods you have foraged. I have even included a few ideas for cooking snails.

The recipes in this book are achievable by everyone. So, whether you live in a city or the countryside, get cooking.

Jean-François Mallet

INTRODUCTION

—

Game has always been the mainstay of a meat diet. Its evolution is linked to that of man, the hunter-gatherer from time immemorial, and its story has brought to life some of the finest chapters in the history of gastronomy.

Today, game, like all wild produce, is only eaten occasionally because in general hunting and foraging have become infrequent pastimes. The time needed for preparation, marinating and cooking, plus the richness of accompaniments that are fulsome and heavy to digest, have driven game out of the kitchens of busy city-dwellers and consigned 'the black meat' to fine dining tables.

Nevertheless, there is no need to live in the country or be an expert hunter to enjoy the taste of game, wild mushrooms and certain berries. Farmers' market stalls, along with some specialist stores and suppliers, will offer these products, when they are in season, of course. Game that's sold in this way will already have been matured. All that remains to be done is to cook it and eat it. And if you are unable to hunt or shoot game yourself, or to find wild game meat at a specialty store, you can always substitute the wild meat with its farm-raised equivalent.

Game meat is prized for its firmness and strength of flavour, which is determined by the animal's lifestyle and diet. Its powerful flavour increases with age and the meat is more dense, deeper in colour, richer in proteins and leaner than the meat of its farm-raised equivalent.

Among my suggested recipes, you will learn how to (re)introduce game and wild produce into an everyday kitchen in a light and refined way, even though the festive and rural connotations attached to game still persist. So what is the secret? I have simplified the preparation and cooking to reveal the true taste of game and wild produce. In recipes that include venison and hare, the meat can be cooked pink or even rare, drizzled with fresh berry sauces made by simply deglazing the pan, and then served with pan-fried chestnuts or vegetables roasted with herbs.

Venison Burgers with Blue Cheese, Purslane and Wild Watercress (page 28), Pheasant and Pine Nut Pastillas (page 107), Hare and Pear Spring Rolls with Blueberry Sauce (page 62) and Wild Mushroom Pizza (page 172), all show just how easily game can be brought up to date.

The great classics, revisited here using creative combinations of ingredients (soy sauce, Parmesan or citrus zests), will once again have you beating a path to your stove, as will such recipes as Daube of Wild Boar with Ceps and Mandarin Zest (page 44), Stewed Hare with Chocolate (page 64), Quails in Red Wine Sauce (page 125) or Fruits of the Forest Clafoutis (page 220). Some must-try pâté recipes are also provided, which are fragrant with spices and enriched with fresh berries or dried fruits.

Wild mushrooms, herbs and fruits are cooked with or without game, in quick and imaginative recipes, such as a Salad of Pied Bleu Mushrooms with Bay Leaves and Thyme (page 157), Nettle Gazpacho with Tomato Bread (page 188) or Wild Strawberries in Blackcurrant and Wine Syrup (page 209).

Game and wild produce form part of that rare group of foods that lead us back through our history, to our connection with nature and our instinct for survival. To rediscover them in the kitchen is also an excellent way to return to our roots and offers us the chance to enjoy the purest of flavours.

A fine wine is the most suitable accompaniment to game.

- For large furred game, choose powerful wines that are full-bodied and have character (Pomerol, Corton, Madiran, Patrimonio, Cahors or a red Côtes-de-Provence);
- for small furred game such as hare, as well as for quail or partridge, some wine waiters recommend a great white wine (Meursault, Tokay or a Pinot Gris from Alsace);
- for all other feathered game, it is preferable to drink a light red wine, such as a Burgundy, whose pinot noir grapes complement the delicate flesh of the game beautifully. You could also serve a red wine from Savoy or a Beaujolais (Moulin-à-Vent or Brouilly).

FURRED GAME

HAUNCH OF VENISON ROASTED WITH COCOA

Serves 6–8

Preparation time:
10 minutes

Cooking time:
35–40 minutes

Resting time:
5–10 minutes

- 1 × 2.5–3 kg/5½–6½ lb haunch of venison (roe deer)
- 1 tablespoon unsweetened cocoa powder
- 2 tablespoons olive oil
- salt and freshly ground pepper
- mashed potatoes, to serve

1.
Preheat the oven to 200°C/400°F/Gas Mark 6.

2.
Put the haunch into a large roasting pan and season with salt and pepper. Dust with the cocoa powder and drizzle over the olive oil. Cook in the oven for 10–15 minutes until the top of the haunch is a good colour. Turn it over, reduce the oven temperature to 170°C/340°F/Gas Mark 3–4 and cook for another 25 minutes, basting the meat occasionally with the cooking juices.

3.
Remove the meat from the oven and leave to rest for 5–10 minutes, then carve into slices. Spoon the cooking juices over the meat slices and serve with mashed potatoes.

NOTE
The haunch is the upper part of the leg of large game. Once the joint has been skinned, it must be dressed, that is to say the fine membrane covering it needs to be removed. Finally, it is important to remove the meat covering the end of the bone and then to weigh the joint to calculate the cooking time, allowing 12–15 minutes per 1 kg/2¼ lb.

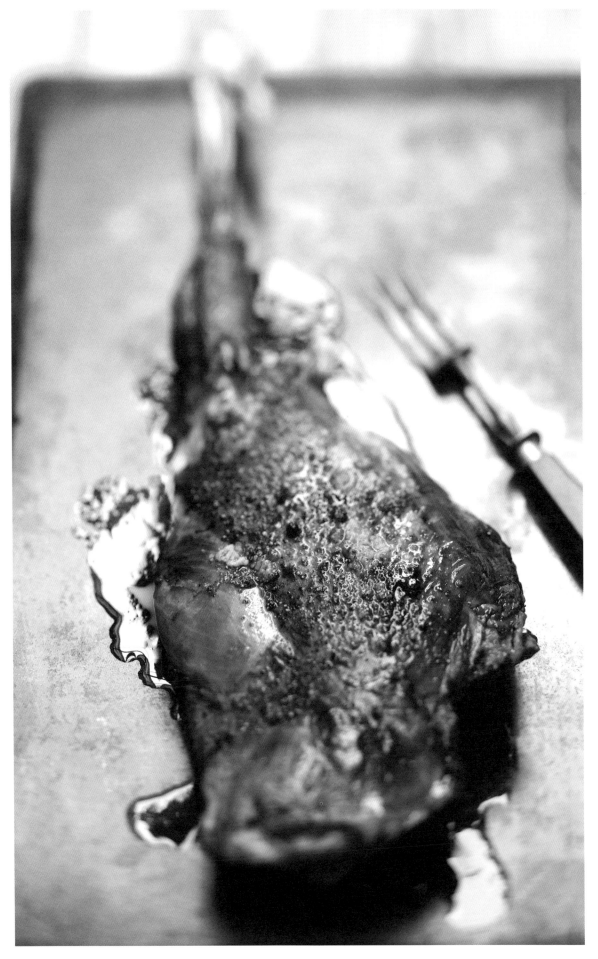

VENISON AND MANGO BROCHETTES

Serves 4

Preparation time:
20 minutes

Cooking time:
15 minutes

- 2 tablespoons olive oil
- 600 g/1 lb 5 oz venison (doe) fillet, cut into cubes
- 4 tablespoons soy sauce
- 2 tablespoons clear (runny) honey
- 2 ripe mangoes, peeled, pitted and cut into chunks
- 1 bunch coriander (cilantro), leaves only
- salt and freshly ground pepper
- cooked white rice, to serve (optional)

1.
Heat the oil in a frying pan or skillet, add the meat and sear over high heat for 5 minutes, or until coloured on all sides, then transfer to a plate and set aside.

2.
Pour the soy sauce into the pan and deglaze by scraping the cooking juices off the bottom of the pan with a wooden spoon or fish slice (spatula) and incorporating them into the soy sauce. Add the honey and cook for 1 minute, or until caramelized. Remove the pan from the heat.

3.
Prepare the brochettes by pushing alternate pieces of meat and mango onto small skewers. Reheat the sauce for 1–2 minutes. Dip the brochettes in the sauce, then remove, drain and arrange them on a bed of the coriander (cilantro) leaves. Season with salt and pepper.

4.
Serve the brochettes hot as a main course with cooked white rice, on their own as a starter (appetizer) or with pre-dinner drinks.

ROLLED HAUNCH OF VENISON WITH WINE

Serves 4

Preparation time:
20 minutes

Cooking time:
4 hours 30 minutes

- 1 × 900-g/2-lb boned haunch of venison (red deer)
- 2 sprigs thyme
- 2 bay leaves
- 4 tablespoons sunflower oil
- 8 cloves garlic, unpeeled and crushed
- 750 ml/25 fl oz (3 cups) dessert wine
- 750 ml/25 fl oz (3 cups) red wine
- 2 carrots
- 50 g/2 oz (4 tablespoons) butter
- salt and freshly ground pepper
- cooked fresh pasta, to serve

1.
Season the haunch with salt and pepper. Place 1 sprig of thyme and 1 bay leaf in the centre of the meat, roll the meat around the herbs and tie up with kitchen string or twine.

2.
Heat the oil in a large flameproof casserole (Dutch oven) over medium-high heat, add the meat and sear for 5–10 minutes until evenly coloured on all sides. Add the garlic, then pour in the dessert wine and deglaze by scraping the cooking juices off the bottom of the casserole with a wooden spoon or fish slice (spatula) and incorporating them into the wine. Simmer for 5 minutes to reduce the liquid by half, then add the red wine and remaining thyme sprig and bay leaf. Reduce the heat to low, cover and simmer for 4 hours, basting the meat occasionally with the cooking juices. There must always be at least 5 cm/2 inches of liquid at the bottom of the casserole, so if the juices reduce too quickly, reduce the heat and add a little water.

3.
Meanwhile, steam or cook the carrots in a saucepan of boiling water for about 15 minutes, or until tender. Drain, place them in a food processor and process until smooth. Add the butter, mix in until combined, then cover to keep the purée hot.

4.
When the haunch is very tender – it should be possible to lift off pieces of meat with a spoon – transfer it carefully to a serving plate. Crush the garlic in the casserole, strain the cooking juices and whisk in the carrot purée. Season with salt and pepper, then spoon the carrot sauce over the meat.

5.
Serve with cooked fresh pasta.

VENISON BURGERS WITH BLUE CHEESE, PURSLANE AND WILD WATERCRESS

Serves 4

Preparation time:
25 minutes

Cooking time:
10 minutes

- 600 g/1 lb 5 oz venison (doe) fillet
- 1 small bunch tarragon, leaves only, chopped
- 3 tablespoons sunflower oil
- 4 burger buns
- 1 tablespoon mustard
- 200 g/7 oz Fourme d'Ambert blue cheese, cut into slices
- 100 g/3½ oz purslane
- 50 g/2 oz wild watercress
- salt and freshly ground pepper

1.
Preheat the oven to 180°C/350°F/Gas Mark 4.

2.
Mince (grind) the meat in a mincer (grinder) and put into a large bowl. Add the tarragon, season with salt and pepper and mix well. Mould the mixture with your hands into 4 evenly sized patties. Set aside.

3.
Heat the oil in a frying pan or skillet over high heat, add the patties and sear for 4 minutes on one side. Turn over and sear for another 4 minutes until cooked. Remove from the pan and set aside on a plate.

4.
Slice the burger buns in half and toast them in the oven until golden. Remove and spread the cut sides of the bottom halves of the buns with the mustard. Place a slice of the cheese on each one, put a meat patty on top, then add another slice of cheese. Top with the bun lids, pressing them down lightly, and put in the oven for 2 minutes.

5.
Remove the cheeseburgers from the oven, add several purslane leaves and watercress sprigs to each one between the cheese and the meat patty and serve.

NOTE
This recipe is proof, if any were needed, that game has more than one trick up its sleeve. These cheeseburgers, made with venison, show how this type of meat lends itself to all kinds of cooking, even the most unexpected.

ROAST VENISON WITH PAIN D'EPICES AND PAN-FRIED CHESTNUTS

Serves 4

Preparation time:
15 minutes

Cooking time:
30–40 minutes

- 1 kg/2¼ lb venison (roe deer) fillet, tied with kitchen string or twine
- 3 tablespoons sunflower oil
- 4 slices pain d'epices or dry gingerbread
- 80 g/3 oz (6 tablespoons) butter
- 500 g/1 lb 2 oz chestnuts, peeled and cooked
- 4 sprigs flat-leaf parsley, leaves only, chopped
- salt and freshly ground pepper

1.
Preheat the oven to 180°C/350°F/Gas Mark 4.

2.
Season the meat with salt and pepper. Heat the oil in a large flameproof casserole (Dutch oven) over high heat, add the meat and sear for 5–10 minutes until coloured on all sides. Transfer to the oven and roast for 20 minutes, or until the meat is cooked.

3.
Remove the meat from the casserole, leaving the cooking juices in the casserole, and leave to rest on a plate, loosely covered with aluminium foil, turning it over occasionally.

4.
Meanwhile, put the pain d'epices or dry gingerbread slices into a food processor and process until crumbs form. Set aside.

5.
Heat the butter in the cooking juices in the casserole, add the chestnuts and stir over medium heat for 5–10 minutes, or until browned. Add three-quarters of the crumbs and the parsley, mix well and pour into a serving dish.

6.
Sprinkle the remaining crumbs over the top of the meat. Carve the meat into thick slices and arrange them over the chestnuts. Spoon over some of the cooking juices to coat the meat and serve.

NOTE
To use fresh chestnuts, cut a cross in the skin of each chestnut with a sharp knife. Heat 3 tablespoons sunflower oil in a large frying pan or skillet and sauté the chestnuts over medium-high heat for 10 minutes, or until golden. Drain and leave until cool enough to handle, then peel off the skins. You can also roast chestnuts over an open fire: they will produce a deliciously smoky aroma that will permeate the whole house. (Make sure you cut a cross in the skins.)

VENISON STEAKS WITH VINEGAR AND CHERRIES

Serves 4

Preparation time:
10 minutes

Cooking time:
15 minutes

Resting time:
5 minutes

- 800 g/1¾ lb venison (roe deer) fillet, cut into 4 evenly sized steaks
- 2 tablespoons olive oil
- 4 tablespoons red wine vinegar
- 400 g/14 oz (2½ cups) cherries (morello or coeur de pigeon), pitted
- 4 tablespoons soy sauce
- 1 bunch tarragon, leaves only, coarsely chopped
- salt and freshly ground pepper
- Celeriac Purée (page 84), to serve

1.

Season the venison steaks with salt and pepper. Heat the oil in a large frying pan or skillet, add the steaks and sear over high heat, turning, until coloured on both sides. Reduce the heat and cook for another 2 minutes. Transfer the steaks to a plate and set aside.

2.

Pour the vinegar into the pan and deglaze by scraping the cooking juices off the bottom of the pan with a wooden spoon or fish slice (spatula) and incorporating them into the vinegar, then simmer for 5 minutes to reduce the liquid by half. Add the cherries, soy sauce and 5 tablespoons water. Bring to the boil, then reduce the heat to low and cook for 3 minutes. Adjust the seasoning, add the tarragon and return the steaks to the pan. Cook for another 1 minute, then remove the pan from the heat and leave the steaks to rest for 5 minutes in the cooking juices.

3.

Serve the venison steaks with celeriac purée.

NOTE

The combination of red fruits and game is a classic. The sweet but acidic flavour of the red fruit provides the perfect balance to the more pronounced flavour of the rich, dark meat.

SMALL VENISON PÂTÉS WITH COCOA

Serves 4

Preparation time:
25 minutes

Cooking time:
1 hour, plus 1 hour cooling

Chilling time:
at least 12 hours

- 500 g/1 lb 2 oz venison (roe deer) meat, cut into pieces
- 200 g/7 oz pork belly (side)
- 2 eggs
- 4 tablespoons unsweetened cocoa powder
- 20 g/¾ oz (about 1 tablespoon) fine salt
- 1 tablespoon freshly ground pepper
- 1 piece pork fat (fatback), chopped into small pieces
- 4 sprigs thyme
- slices of toasted brioche, to serve

1.
Mince (grind) the venison and pork belly (side) through a mincer (grinder) and put into a large bowl. Add the eggs, cocoa powder, salt and pepper and mix together with your hands until combined.

2.
Preheat the oven to 170°C/340°F/Gas Mark 3–4.

3.
Put a few pieces of the pork fat (fatback) in the bottom of 4 small ramekins. Add the minced meat mixture, packing it down firmly, and top with the remaining pieces of pork fat and the thyme sprigs. Put the ramekins into a large ovenproof dish and carefully pour hot water into the dish to come halfway up the sides of the ramekins to create a bain-marie. Cook in the oven for 1 hour.

4.
When the pâtés are cooked, remove from the oven and leave to cool for 1 hour at room temperature, then chill in the refrigerator for at least 12 hours before eating.

5.
Serve with slices of toasted brioche.

VENISON FILLET WRAPPED IN CABBAGE LEAVES WITH BERRY SAUCE

Serves 4

Preparation time:
25 minutes

Cooking time:
25 minutes

- 4 green cabbage leaves, white stalk removed
- 900 g/2 lb venison (roe deer) fillet, cut into 4 evenly sized pieces
- 3 tablespoons sunflower oil
- 100 ml/3½ fl oz (scant ½ cup) veal stock (broth)
- 100 g/3½ oz (⅔ cup) blueberries
- 5 bunches redcurrants, removed from their stalks
- 5 blackberries
- 50 g/2 oz (scant ½ cup) blackcurrants
- salt and freshly ground pepper
- mashed potatoes, to serve

1.
Blanch the cabbage leaves for 10 minutes in a saucepan of boiling water. Drain, plunge them immediately into cold water and then drain again.

2.
Season the venison with salt and pepper, then place each piece on a cabbage leaf. Roll the leaf around the meat, folding in the sides as you roll. Tie the packages neatly with kitchen string or twine so they keep their shape.

3.
Heat the oil in a large flameproof casserole (Dutch oven) over high heat, add the cabbage packages and sear for 3 minutes until coloured. Reduce the heat and cook for 5 minutes, turning the packages over occasionally. Transfer to a plate, cover with aluminium foil and leave to rest.

4.
Deglaze the casserole with the stock (broth) by scraping the cooking juices off the bottom of the casserole with a wooden spoon or fish slice (spatula) and incorporating them into the stock. Simmer for about 5 minutes to reduce the liquid by three-quarters. Add all the fruits, bring to the boil, season with salt and pepper and remove from the heat.

5.
Remove the kitchen string and cut the cabbage packages into slices and serve with the berry sauce and mashed potatoes.

NOTE
Dark red roe deer flesh is tender and very tasty, especially the meat from young animals. As such, there is no need to marinate it. After cooking, the meat should still be pink in the centre.

SAUTÉED VENISON WITH PORT AND CHESTNUTS

Serves 4

Preparation time:
10 minutes

Cooking time:
2 hours 15 minutes

- 1 × 900-g/2-lb haunch of venison (roe deer), cut into large cubes
- 4 tablespoons sunflower oil
- 1 large onion, chopped
- 150 ml/5 fl oz (⅔ cup) ruby port
- 1 tablespoon plain (all-purpose) flour
- 2 sprigs thyme
- 2 bay leaves
- 500 ml/17 fl oz (generous 2 cups) veal stock (broth)
- 80 g/3 oz (6 tablespoons) butter
- 500 g/1 lb 2 oz chestnuts, peeled and pre-cooked
- salt and freshly ground pepper

1.

Season the meat with salt and pepper. Heat the oil in a large flameproof casserole (Dutch oven) over high heat, add the meat and sear for 5 minutes until coloured all over. Add the onion and fry for another 5 minutes until browned.

2.

Deglaze the casserole with the port by scraping the cooking juices off the bottom of the casserole with a wooden spoon or fish slice (spatula) and incorporating them into the port, then simmer for 5 minutes to reduce the liquid by half. Add the flour, thyme and bay leaves and mix in. Pour in the stock (broth), reduce the heat to low and simmer for 2 hours.

3.

After 1 hour of cooking, melt the butter in another casserole over medium heat, add the chestnuts, reduce the heat to very low and cook for 1 hour, stirring occasionally.

4.

When the meat is cooked, adjust the seasoning, if necessary, and remove the bay leaves. Stir in the chestnuts and serve immediately.

TIP

If you have fresh chestnuts, you can prepare them yourself according to the instructions on page 30.

FILLET OF VENISON EN CROUTE WITH BLUEBERRY SAUCE

Serves 4

Preparation time:
10 minutes

Cooking time:
35–40 minutes, plus cooling time

Resting time:
10 minutes

- 900 g/2 lb venison (doe) fillet
- 2 tablespoons sunflower oil
- 100 ml/3½ fl oz (scant ½ cup) veal stock (broth), optional
- 150 g/5 oz (1 cup) blueberries
- 1 egg yolk
- 1 sheet ready-rolled all-butter puff pastry
- salt and freshly ground pepper
- salad or pan-fried mushrooms, to serve

1.
Season the venison with salt and pepper.

2.
Heat the oil in a large flameproof casserole (Dutch oven) over high heat, add the meat and sear for 5–10 minutes until evenly coloured all over. Remove the meat from the casserole, place it on a wire rack and leave to cool completely.

3.
Pour the stock (broth) or 100 ml/3½ fl oz (scant ½ cup) water into the casserole and deglaze by scraping the cooking juices off the bottom of the casserole with a wooden spoon or fish slice (spatula) and incorporating them into the stock, then simmer for about 5 minutes to reduce the liquid by half.

4.
Add the blueberries to the casserole, season with salt and pepper and simmer for 5 minutes over low heat. Remove from the heat.

5.
Preheat the oven to 200°C/400°F/Gas Mark 6 and line a large baking sheet with baking parchment.

6.
Beat the egg yolk in a small bowl with a little water. Unroll the puff pastry dough onto a work counter and place the venison on top, on one side. Lift up the empty side of the pastry and fold over the venison. Seal the pastry with some of the beaten egg and press the edges together firmly. Allow some overlap but trim away any excess pastry. Lift the pastry-wrapped roast onto the prepared baking sheet, placing it seam-side down. Using a brush, glaze the pastry with the beaten egg and cook in the oven for 20 minutes, or until the pastry is a rich golden colour.

7.
Remove from the oven and let rest for 10 minutes. Meanwhile, reheat the sauce.

7.
Cut the venison en croute into thick slices and serve with the blueberry sauce and a salad or some pan-fried mushrooms.

GAME TURNOVER

Serves 4

Preparation time:
15 minutes

Cooking time:
35 minutes

- 1 egg yolk
- 1 sheet ready-rolled all-butter puff pastry
- 400 g/14 oz (3 cups) cold leftover game ragoût, such as wild boar ragoût (page 50 or 54)
- salt and freshly ground pepper
- green salad, to serve

1.
Preheat the oven to 180°C/350°F/Gas Mark 4 and line a baking sheet with baking parchment.

2.
Beat the egg yolk in a small bowl with 1 teaspoon cold water.

3.
Unroll the puff pastry dough on the prepared baking sheet. Spoon the leftover game ragoût in the centre and season with salt and pepper, if necessary. Fold the pastry around the filling and seal the edges by pressing them together with a fork. Glaze the pastry by brushing with the beaten egg, then bake in the oven for 35 minutes.

4.
When the turnover is cooked, remove from the oven and leave to cool a little before serving with a green salad.

FURRED GAME

DRY-CURED WILD BOAR SAUSAGES

Makes 4 sausages

Preparation time:
20 minutes

Drying time:
3 weeks

- 1.5 kg/3¼ lb wild boar meat
- 700 g/1 lb 8½ oz pork fat
  (fatback)
- 2 teaspoons coarsely ground
  pepper
- 60 g/2¼ oz (scant ⅓ cup)
  fine salt
- 5 g/⅛ oz (1 teaspoon) curing
  salt mix (available from a
  pork butcher or chemist,
  see page 225)
- 1 teaspoon caster (superfine)
  sugar
- 1.2 m/4 feet pig casings
  (available from a butcher),
  soaked, rinsed and cut into
  30-cm/12-inch lengths

1.
Coarsely mince (grind) the meat and pork fat (fatback) in a mincer (grinder) and put into a large bowl. Season the meat with the pepper, salt, curing salt mix and sugar and mix together with your hands until combined.

2.
Take a length of casing and tie one of the ends closed with a simple knot. Carefully fill the casing with a quarter of the meat mixture, packing it in tightly, and close the other end by twisting it and tying with a knot. Repeat with the remaining casings until all the meat mixture has been used.

3.
Hang the sausages up on hooks and leave to dry for 3 weeks in an airy and relatively dry room.

TIP
These sausages can be stored in a dry and airy place for several months. You can make sausages in the same way using venison (roe deer) meat.

DAUBE OF WILD BOAR WITH CEPS AND MANDARIN ZEST

Serves 4

Preparation time:
30 minutes

Cooking time:
2 hours 20 minutes

- 4 tablespoons olive oil
- 1 × 900-g/2-lb haunch of wild boar, cut into small chunks
- 4 cloves garlic, crushed
- 1 large onion, chopped
- 1 tablespoon plain (all-purpose) flour
- 750 ml/25 fl oz (3 cups) red wine
- 1 sprig thyme
- 1 bay leaf
- grated zest and juice of 6 organic mandarins
- 6 large ceps (porcini), cut into thick slices (see note)
- salt and freshly ground pepper
- cooked fresh pasta, to serve

1.
Heat 2 tablespoons of the oil in a large flameproof casserole (Dutch oven) over medium-high heat, add the meat and sear for 5 minutes, or until coloured all over. Add the garlic and onion and fry for another 3–5 minutes until browned, then add the flour and mix until the meat is well coated. Pour in the red wine, add the thyme and bay leaf and the mandarin zest and juice. Reduce the heat to very low and simmer for 2 hours, stirring occasionally.

2.
Heat the remaining oil in a large frying pan or skillet over medium-high heat, add the ceps (porcini) and fry for 5 minutes, or until coloured. Set aside.

3.
When the meat is cooked and meltingly tender, remove the bay leaf, add the ceps, stir until mixed in and season with salt and pepper.

4.
Serve with cooked fresh pasta.

NOTE
To prepare the ceps, scrape the earth from the mushrooms, then rinse in a sieve (strainer) under cold running water and dry. See A Note on Mushrooms (page 239).

ROAST WILD BOAR WITH DRIED FRUITS AND PORT

Serves 4

Preparation time:
5 minutes

Cooking time:
1 hour 10 minutes

- 1 × 900-g/2-lb roasting joint
  of wild boar, off the bone,
  tied up with kitchen string
  or twine
- 2 tablespoons sunflower oil
- 50 ml/1¾ fl oz (scant ¼ cup)
  white port
- 2 tablespoons sherry vinegar
- 5 dried apricots
- 8 prunes (dried plums)
  or dried figs, halved
- 25 blanched almonds
- 25 hazelnuts
- 2 tablespoons clear
  (runny) honey
- salt and freshly ground pepper
- Celeriac Purée (page 84),
  to serve

1.

Season the meat with salt and pepper. Heat the oil in a flameproof casserole (Dutch oven) over high heat, add the meat and sear for 5–10 minutes until coloured on all sides. Reduce the heat to low, pour in the port and vinegar and simmer for 5 minutes to reduce the liquid. Add the apricots, prunes (dried plums), almonds and hazelnuts, then pour in 200 ml/7 fl oz (scant 1 cup) water. Cover and cook over very low heat for 40 minutes, basting the meat occasionally with the cooking juices.

2.

When the meat is cooked, remove it, along with the fruits and nuts, from the casserole with a slotted spoon and put onto a plate. Leave the cooking juices over the heat to reduce slightly. Add the honey and cook for about 5 minutes until caramelized. Return the meat and dried fruits and nuts to the casserole and reheat for 3 minutes until hot.

3.

Remove the meat with a slotted spoon and carve it into thick slices. Serve with the fruits, nuts, sauce and celeriac purée.

SPICED WILD
BOAR PÂTÉ

Serves 4

Preparation time:
25 minutes

Cooking time:
1 hour 30 minutes, plus
   1 hour cooling

Chilling time:
at least 12 hours

- 1 kg/2¼ lb wild boar meat, cut
  into pieces
- 300 g/11 oz pork belly (side)
- 2 eggs
- 20 g/¾ oz (about 1 tablespoon)
  fine salt
- 4 tablespoons freshly ground
  pepper
- 1 tablespoon curry powder
- 1 teaspoon ground cumin
- 150 g/5 oz pork fat (fatback)

To serve:
- salad of dandelion leaves
  (greens)
- slices of toasted bread
- olive oil, to drizzle

1.
Preheat the oven to 160°C/325°F/Gas Mark 3.

2.
Mince (grind) the meat and pork belly (side) in a mincer (grinder) and put into a large bowl. Add the eggs, salt, pepper and spices and mix with your hands until combined.

3.
Put the piece of pork fat (fatback) into the bottom of a terrine dish or loaf pan and top with the meat mixture, pressing it down firmly. Cook in the oven for 1 hour 30 minutes, or until cooked.

4.
Remove the pâté from the oven and leave to cool for 1 hour at room temperature, then chill in the refrigerator for at least 12 hours before eating.

5.
Serve the pâté cut into slices with a salad of dandelion leaves (greens), slices of toasted bread and a drizzle of olive oil.

SMALL WILD BOAR PIES

Serves 6

Preparation time:
20 minutes

Cooking time:
3 hours 20 minutes, plus
    cooling time

Chilling time:
12 hours

- 1 kg/2¼ lb wild boar meat, cut
  into large cubes
- 50 g/2 oz (4 tablespoons) butter
- 2 tablespoons sunflower oil
- 1 large onion, chopped
- 1 bay leaf
- 1 tablespoon plain
  (all-purpose) flour
- 500 ml/17 fl oz (generous
  2 cups) veal stock (broth)
- 2 egg yolks
- 1 sheet ready-rolled all-butter
  puff pastry
- salt and freshly ground pepper
- 6 sprigs thyme, to decorate
  (optional)

1.

The night before, season the meat with salt and pepper.

2.

Heat the butter and oil in a large flameproof casserole (Dutch oven) over medium-high heat. When the butter has melted, add the meat and sear for 5–10 minutes until coloured on all sides. Add the onion and bay leaf and fry for another 5 minutes until browned. Add the flour and pour in the stock (broth) so that it isn't dry. Reduce the heat and simmer for 5–10 minutes to reduce the liquid by half. Pour in 400 ml/14 fl oz (1⅔ cups) water and simmer for 2 hours over low heat, stirring occasionally until the meat is cooked and very tender.

3.

Remove the casserole from the heat, remove the bay leaf and adjust the seasoning. Leave to cool at room temperature, then chill in the refrigerator for 12 hours.

4.

The next day, preheat the oven to 200°C/400°F/Gas Mark 6.

5.

Beat the egg yolks in a small bowl with 2 teaspoons water. Unroll the puff pastry dough onto a work counter and, using a pastry (cookie) cutter, cut out 6 rounds of pastry slightly larger than the tops of the ramekins in which you are going to cook the pies. Divide the wild boar ragoût among the ramekins, then brush the rims of the ramekins with the beaten egg mix and cover each one with a round of puff pastry. Glaze the pastry lids by brushing them with a little more of the egg mixture. Bake the pies in the oven for 1 hour, making sure the pastry doesn't burn.

6.

Decorate each pie with a sprig of thyme and serve immediately in the ramekins.

WILD BOAR WRAPPED IN GREEN CHARD LEAVES

Serves 4

Preparation time:
30 minutes

Cooking time:
35 minutes

- 800 g/1¾ lb wild boar meat, preferably from the leg, cut into pieces
- 200 g/7 oz pork belly (side)
- 15 g/½ oz (2½ teaspoons) salt
- 2 teaspoons freshly ground pepper
- 4 sprigs parsley, leaves only, chopped
- 1 bunch tarragon, leaves only, chopped
- 3 mint leaves, chopped
- 4 large green (Swiss) chard leaves
- 4 tablespoons olive oil

1.
Mince (grind) the wild boar meat and pork belly (side) in a mincer (grinder) and put into a large bowl. Season with the salt and pepper, add the herbs and mix with your hands until combined. Set aside.

2.
Carefully remove the thick white parts of the (Swiss) chard leaves. Blanch the green parts of the leaves for 2 minutes in a saucepan of boiling salted water. Drain and immediately plunge them into a bowl of cold water and drain again.

3.
Preheat the oven to 170°C/340°F/Gas Mark 3–4.

4.
Lay the chard leaves on a work counter and cut each one in half. Spoon the stuffing onto the leaves and wrap them around the stuffing, moulding them into neat packages in the hollow of your hand. Place the packages in a large gratin dish, drizzle with the oil and cook in the oven for 35 minutes. Serve hot or cold.

WILD BOAR RAGOÛT WITH LENTILS AND TARRAGON

Serves 4

Preparation time:
15 minutes

Cooking time:
2 hours 15 minutes, plus
    cooling time

- 400 g/14 oz (2 cups) Puy (French green) lentils
- 1 bay leaf
- 4 tablespoons sunflower oil
- 1 kg/2¼ lb wild boar meat, preferably from the leg, cut into large cubes
- 1 large onion, chopped
- 1 clove garlic, chopped
- 250 ml/8 fl oz (1 cup) red wine
- 250 ml/8 fl oz (1 cup) veal stock (broth)
- 1 bunch tarragon, leaves only, coarsely chopped
- salt and freshly ground pepper

1.

Put the lentils and bay leaf into a large saucepan. Pour in enough water to cover and bring to the boil. Reduce the heat and simmer over medium heat for 20–25 minutes until soft. Add more water if it looks like the lentils are becoming dry. Remove the pan from the heat and leave the lentils to cool in their cooking water until they break up.

2.

Heat the oil in a large flameproof casserole (Dutch oven) over high heat, add the meat and sear for 5 minutes until coloured on all sides. Add the onion and garlic and cook for another 5 minutes, or until browned. Pour in the red wine and simmer to reduce the liquid by three-quarters. Pour in the stock (broth), reduce the heat to low and simmer for 1 hour 30 minutes, or until the meat is tender.

3.

Drain the lentils, remove the bay leaf, and add the lentils to the casserole with the tarragon. Cook for 5 minutes over low heat. Season with salt and pepper and serve.

CABBAGE STUFFED WITH GAME

Serves 4–6

Preparation time:
35 minutes

Cooking time:
2 hours

- 800 g/1¾ lb game meat (pieces from different types of game), cut into pieces
- 200 ml/7 fl oz (scant 1 cup) single (light) cream
- 2 eggs
- 4 litres/136 fl oz (14 cups) beef stock (broth)
- 1 small green cabbage
- salt and freshly ground pepper
- 4 tablespoons walnut oil

1.
Put the meat into a food processor and process, incorporating the cream, then the eggs, one at a time. Season with salt and pepper and blend until it is a fine stuffing with an even texture.

2.
Heat the stock (broth) in a large stew pan (stockpot).

3.
Meanwhile, cut off the cabbage stalk and discard any tough outer leaves. Wash the cabbage in plenty of water, making sure to remove any dirt. Remove the small heart in the centre of the cabbage, wash, chop and mix it into the stuffing.

4.
Fill the centre of the cabbage with the stuffing and cover with the cabbage leaves so the stuffing is hidden. Wrap the cabbage in a clean cloth. Tie the cloth firmly with kitchen string or twine and lower it into the hot stock. Cook for 2 hours, keeping the heat low so the stock is just trembling on the surface.

5.
Drain the cabbage, cut it into large wedges and serve piping hot, drizzled with the walnut oil.

TIP
If the stew pan is sufficiently deep, you can place a wooden spoon across the top of it and suspend the cabbage from the spoon while it cooks, thus avoiding the cabbage being crushed against the bottom of the pan.

NOTE
This kind of recipe is a good way of using up pieces of game that have not been cooked.

SADDLES OF HARE WITH DANDELION SALAD AND TREVISO

Serves 4

Preparation time:
20 minutes

Cooking time:
15 minutes

- 2 saddles of hare
- 6 tablespoons olive oil
- 2 tablespoons red wine vinegar
- 1 head of Treviso radicchio,
  cut into thick slices
- 200 g/7 oz (4 cups) dandelion
  leaves (greens), see note
  on page 185
- salt and freshly ground pepper

1.
Using a very sharp knife, remove the fillets from the saddles of hare (you can ask your butcher to do this for you), then season with salt and pepper.

2.
Mix 4 tablespoons of the olive oil with the vinegar in a small bowl and set aside.

3.
Heat the remaining 2 tablespoons of oil in a large frying pan or skillet over high heat, add the hare fillets and sear for 5 minutes until coloured all over. Reduce the heat to medium and cook for another 5 minutes. Remove the fillets from the pan with a slotted spoon and place on a plate. Set aside.

4.
Deglaze the pan with the oil and vinegar mixture by scraping the cooking juices off the bottom of the pan with a wooden spoon or fish slice (spatula) and incorporating them into the mixture, then simmer for 5 minutes to reduce the liquid. Add the Treviso radicchio, stir, then remove from the heat so that the salad leaves stay crisp.

5.
Put the dandelion leaves (greens) into a salad bowl, add the warm vinaigrette and Treviso radicchio from the pan and mix together. Carve the hare fillets into slices and arrange them over the salad, adding the juices that have run out of the meat. Serve immediately.

NOTE
When using dandelion leaves, be sure to wash them very well and dry in a salad spinner before eating.

DAUBE OF HARE WITH GOLDEN CHANTERELLES AND WALNUTS

Serves 4

Preparation time:
30 minutes

Cooking time:
1 hour 25 minutes

- 1 hare, cut into pieces (see note)
- 3 tablespoons olive oil
- 2 thick slices smoked pork belly (side), cut into lardons
- 1 large onion, chopped
- 2 cloves garlic, chopped
- 1 sprig thyme
- 2 bay leaves
- 750 ml/25 fl oz (3 cups) red wine
- 250 ml/8 fl oz (1 cup) veal stock (broth)
- 400 g/14 oz golden chanterelle mushrooms
- 50 g/2 oz (4 tablespoons) butter
- 10 walnuts, shelled and chopped
- salt and freshly ground pepper
- cooked fresh pasta or polenta, to serve

1.
Season the hare with salt and pepper. Heat the oil in a large flameproof casserole (Dutch oven) over high heat, add the hare and sear for 5 minutes, or until coloured on all sides. Add the pork lardons, onion, garlic, thyme and bay leaves and cook for another 5–10 minutes until browned. Pour in the red wine and simmer for 10 minutes, or until it is reduced by half. Pour in the stock (broth), reduce the heat to very low and simmer for 1 hour, stirring occasionally.

2.
Meanwhile, quickly rinse the golden chanterelles in a sieve (strainer), dry and cut off the gritty base of the stalks.

3.
Melt the butter in a frying pan or skillet, add the golden chanterelles and fry over medium heat for 5 minutes. Add the chopped walnuts and stir until mixed, then remove the pan from the heat.

4.
When the hare is completely cooked, remove the bay leaves, add the golden chanterelles and walnuts to the casserole and adjust the seasoning, if necessary. Serve with cooked fresh pasta or polenta.

NOTE
The flesh of a hare is lean. Depending on the age of the animal, it needs to be cooked in different ways. A young hare (from 2–4 months) is roasted, and the saddle of a year-old hare (up to 1 year) can be roasted or sautéed. Older than 1 year, the meat should be cooked as jugged hare (page 68). In the kitchen, a year-old hare is considered to be the best.

HARE AND PEAR SPRING ROLLS WITH BLUEBERRY SAUCE

Serves 4

Preparation time:
35 minutes

Cooking time:
15 minutes

- 2 saddles of hare
- 5 tablespoons olive oil
- 4 tablespoons soy sauce
- 50 g/2 oz (⅓ cup) blueberries
- 2 sprigs coriander (cilantro), leaves only (optional)
- 3 ripe pears
- 8 rice spring roll wrappers
- 8 mint leaves
- 8 Thai basil leaves (available from Asian food stores)
- 5 sprigs tarragon, leaves only
- salt and freshly ground pepper

1.

Using a very sharp knife, remove the fillets from the saddles of hare (you can ask your butcher to do this for you), then season with salt and pepper.

2.

Heat 2 tablespoons of the olive oil in a large frying pan or skillet over high heat, add the hare fillets and sear for about 5 minutes, or until coloured all over. Reduce the heat to medium and cook for another 5 minutes. Remove the fillets from the pan with a slotted spoon and transfer to a plate. Keep warm.

3.

Deglaze the pan with the soy sauce by scraping the cooking juices off the bottom of the pan with a wooden spoon or fish slice (spatula) and incorporating them into the soy sauce. Simmer for 5 minutes to reduce the liquid. Add the blueberries and cook for 1 minute, then remove the pan from the heat. Add the remaining olive oil and stir in until combined. Add the coriander (cilantro), if using, transfer to a bowl and set aside.

4.

Cut the hare fillets into thin slices. Peel the pears, remove the cores and cut them into thin wedges.

5.

Lightly brush the spring roll wrappers with water until damp. Lay them on a work counter and pile the herbs, pear wedges and slices of meat in the centre. Fold the sides of the wrappers in over the filling and roll up. Place the spring rolls in the refrigerator for 5 minutes, then serve with the blueberry sauce.

STEWED HARE
WITH CHOCOLATE

Serves 4

Preparation time:
20 minutes

Cooking time:
2 hours 20 minutes

- 1 hare, cut into pieces
- 2 tablespoons olive oil
- 4 shallots, finely chopped
- 750 ml/25 fl oz (3 cups) red wine
- 300 ml/10 fl oz (1¼ cups) dessert wine
- 2 squares (about 10 g/¼ oz) dark (bittersweet) chocolate
- salt and freshly ground pepper
- cooked fresh pasta or mashed potatoes, to serve

1.

Season the hare with salt and pepper. Heat the oil in a large flameproof casserole (Dutch oven) over high heat, add the meat and sear for 5 minutes until evenly coloured all over. Add the shallots and cook for another 5 minutes. Pour in the red wine and dessert wine, reduce the heat to low and cook for 2 hours, uncovered.

2.

Lift the hare out of the casserole with a slotted spoon, remove the bones and pull all the meat off them. Leave the cooking juices over the heat to reduce until thickened a little. Add the chocolate squares and whisk them into the juices until they melt, then remove from the heat. Adjust the seasoning, if necessary, return the meat to the casserole and reheat for 3 minutes until hot.

3.

Serve immediately with cooked fresh pasta or mashed potatoes.

NOTE

At first, the combination of game and chocolate might seem surprising but it is, nevertheless, common in game cooking. The chocolate adds subtlety and smoothness to the sauce without becoming dominant. It also mellows the flavour of the game.

FURRED GAME

HARE PÂTÉ
WITH THYME

Serves 4

Preparation time:
25 minutes

Cooking time:
1 hour, plus 1 hour cooling

Chilling time:
at least 12 hours

- 4 hare leg joints, boned
- 400 g/14 oz pork belly (side)
- 4 sprigs thyme, leaves
  only, chopped, plus extra
  sprigs, to decorate (optional)
- 1 egg, beaten
- 2 teaspoons salt
- 1 teaspoon coarsely
  ground pepper
- 1 piece pork fat (fatback),
  chopped into strips

1.
Preheat the oven to 180°C/350°F/Gas Mark 4.

2.
Coarsely mince (grind) the hare meat and pork belly (side) in
a mincer (grinder) and put into a large bowl. Add the thyme,
beaten egg, salt and pepper and mix together with your hands
until combined.

3.
Put the mixture into a terrine dish or loaf pan, packing it down
firmly. Top with the strips of pork fat (fatback). Lift the terrine
into an ovenproof dish and carefully pour hot water into the dish
to come halfway up the sides of the terrine to create a bain-marie.
Cook in the oven for 1 hour.

4.
When the pâté is cooked, remove from the oven and leave to cool
for 1 hour at room temperature, then chill in the refrigerator for
at least 12 hours before serving.

5.
Decorate with sprigs of thyme, if using, before serving.

JUGGED HARE WITH RED CABBAGE

Serves 4–6

Preparation time:
30 minutes

Cooking time:
2 hours 15 minutes

- 1 large hare (1.8–2 kg/4–4½ lb), cut into pieces (ask your butcher to keep the blood for you)
- 4 tablespoons sunflower oil
- 200 g/7 oz bacon lardons (optional)
- 2 tablespoons Armagnac or Cognac
- 1 tablespoon plain (all-purpose) flour
- 2 carrots, chopped into small pieces
- 1 onion, chopped into small pieces
- 2 bay leaves
- 1 litre/34 fl oz (4¼ cups) red wine
- 80 g/3 oz (6 tablespoons) butter
- ½ red cabbage, finely sliced
- 50 g/2 oz (⅓ cup) raisins
- 1 square (about 5 g/⅛ oz) dark (bittersweet) chocolate, chopped
- salt and freshly ground pepper

To serve:
- Celeriac Purée (page 84)
- croûtons of bread cubes fried in butter until golden

1.
Season the hare with salt and pepper. Heat the oil in a large flameproof casserole (Dutch oven) over high heat, add the hare and sear for 5–10 minutes until coloured all over. Add the bacon lardons, if using, then pour in the Armagnac or Cognac, heat for a few moments and set alight. When the flames have extinguished, add the flour, stirring until mixed in, then add the carrots, onion and bay leaves. Reduce the heat to very low, pour in the red wine, cover and simmer for 2 hours.

2.
After 1 hour 30 minutes, melt 50 g/2 oz (4 tablespoons) of the butter in a large frying pan or skillet until foaming, then add the red cabbage and raisins and cook for 25 minutes over low heat.

3.
Spoon the cabbage onto a large serving platter. Lift the hare out of the casserole and arrange the meat over the red cabbage.

4.
Bring the sauce in the casserole to the boil, then remove from the heat. Add the remaining 30 g/1 oz (2 tablespoons) butter and the chocolate and whisk until melted. Pour in the hare's blood and adjust the seasoning, if necessary.

5.
Strain the sauce through a sieve (strainer), then spoon it over the hare and cabbage. Serve with celeriac purée and croûtons.

NOTE
The hare blood thickens the sauce and adds depth and flavour. Take care, because after it has been poured in, the sauce must not boil again.

WILD RABBIT, TARRAGON AND MUSTARD TERRINE

Serves 4

Preparation time:
20 minutes

Cooking time:
1 hour, plus 1 hour cooling

Chilling time:
at least 12 hours

- 1 wild rabbit, boned
- 300 g/11 oz pork belly (side)
- 4 tablespoons hot mustard
- 2 eggs
- 1 teaspoon dried thyme
- 4 sprigs tarragon, reserve
  1 sprig and coarsely chop
  the rest
- 20 g/¾ oz (about 1 tablespoon)
  salt
- 1 tablespoon coarsely
  crushed pepper
- 1 piece pork fat (fatback)

To serve:
- slices of toasted rustic bread
- rocket (arugula) salad

1.

Preheat the oven to 180°C/350°F/Gas Mark 4.

2.

Mince (grind) the rabbit meat and pork belly (side) in a mincer (grinder) and put into a large bowl. Add the mustard, eggs, thyme, chopped tarragon, salt and pepper and mix together with your hands until combined.

3.

Place the pork fat (fatback) in the bottom of a terrine dish and spoon in the meat mixture, packing it down firmly. Lay the reserved tarragon sprig on top. Put the terrine into a large ovenproof dish, then carefully pour hot water into the dish to come halfway up the sides of the terrine to create a bain-marie. Cook in the oven for 1 hour.

4.

When the terrine is cooked, remove from the oven and leave to cool for 1 hour at room temperature, then chill in the refrigerator for at least 12 hours before eating.

5.

Serve the wild rabbit terrine with slices of toasted rustic bread and a rocket (arugula) salad.

WILD RABBIT PACKAGES WITH SAGE AND SQUASH

Serves 4

Preparation time:
35 minutes

Cooking time:
35 minutes

- 1 wild rabbit, boned
- 10 sage leaves, 5 left whole and 5 chopped
- 8 small, very thin veal escalopes (scallops)
- 8 thin rashers (slices) smoked bacon
- 70 g/2¾ oz (5 tablespoons) butter
- 1 tablespoon sunflower oil
- 2 onion squashes or red kuri squashes, cut into 5-cm/2-inch wedges and de-seeded
- salt and freshly ground pepper

1.
Mince (grind) the rabbit meat in a mincer (grinder) and put into a large bowl. Add the chopped sage, season with salt and pepper and mix together with your hands.

2.
Lay the veal escalopes (scallops) on a work counter, place a little of the rabbit stuffing in the centre of each and enclose the stuffing by wrapping the escalopes around it. Wrap the bacon rashers (slices) around the packages and tie neatly with kitchen string or twine to secure.

3.
Preheat the oven to 180°C/350°F/Gas Mark 4.

4.
Melt the butter and oil in a large flameproof casserole (Dutch oven) over high heat, add the packages and sear for 5 minutes, turning, until coloured all over. Add the whole sage leaves and the squash wedges, then cover and cook in the oven for about 25 minutes.

5.
When the packages are cooked, transfer them to a serving plate and spoon the cooking juices over them. Serve hot with the pumpkin wedges.

FURRED GAME

WHOLE WILD RABBIT ROASTED WITH AROMATIC HERBS

Serves 4

Preparation time:
10 minutes

Cooking time:
45 minutes

- 1 whole young wild rabbit, gutted and cleaned
- 2 sprigs rosemary
- 2 sprigs thyme
- 2 sprigs wild thyme
- 2 sprigs oregano
- 1 tablespoon olive oil
- 2 tablespoons clear (runny) honey
- 2 tablespoons soy sauce
- salt and freshly ground pepper
- mashed potatoes, to serve

1.
Preheat the oven to 170°C/340°F/Gas Mark 3–4.

2.
Season the rabbit with salt and pepper, then stuff it with half the herbs and tie neatly with kitchen string or twine. Put the rabbit into a roasting dish and drizzle with the olive oil. Roast in the oven for 45 minutes, checking to see when the rabbit begins to colour, then brush with the honey and soy sauce and baste frequently as it cooks.

3.
Arrange the remaining herbs on a serving platter and place the cooked rabbit on top. Drizzle with the cooking juices and serve with mashed potatoes.

NOTE
Wild rabbit meat is pale pink, very tender and contains very little fat. It goes extremely well with aromatic herbs and spices. Young rabbits are kept for roasting, casseroling or to be cooked as a stew (jugged), while older rabbits are made into flavoursome terrines.

WILD RABBIT CASSEROLE WITH WILD GARLIC AND FRESH ALMONDS

Serves 4

Preparation time:
10 minutes

Cooking time:
1 hour

- 3 tablespoons sunflower oil
- 1 large wild rabbit, cut into pieces
- 2 tablespoons clear (runny) honey
- 1 clove wild garlic, crushed
- 500 ml/17 fl oz (generous 2 cups) white wine
- 5 wild garlic leaves (greens), finely chopped
- 200 g/7 oz (1⅓ cups) fresh almonds, shelled
- salt and freshly ground pepper
- cooked fresh pasta, to serve

1.

Heat the oil in a large flameproof casserole (Dutch oven) over high heat, add the rabbit and sear for 5 minutes, or until coloured all over. Reduce the heat, add the honey and garlic and cook for 5–10 minutes until caramelized. The sauce base must be light brown. Pour in the wine and reduce the heat to low. Season with salt and pepper, cover and cook for about 30 minutes.

2.

Add the chopped wild garlic leaves (greens) and almonds to the casserole and cook for another 15 minutes.

3.

Season the cooked rabbit with salt and pepper and serve immediately with cooked fresh pasta.

PECORINO PASTA WITH GAME SAUCE

Serves 4

Preparation time:
10 minutes

Cooking time:
25 minutes

- 400 g/14 oz rigatoni (long, ridged pasta tubes)
- 4 tablespoons olive oil
- 2 cloves pink garlic, chopped
- 500 g/1 lb 2 oz (3 cups) leftover wild boar (page 50 or 54), venison (roe deer) or hare ragoût
- 50 g/2 oz (scant ½ cup) pecorino cheese, coarsely crumbled, plus extra shavings to garnish
- 10 basil leaves, coarsely chopped
- salt and freshly ground pepper

1.
Cook the rigatoni pasta in a large saucepan of boiling, salted water for 10–12 minutes, or according to package directions, until al dente. Drain, reserving a little of the cooking water, and set aside.

2.
Heat the oil in a large sauté pan, add the garlic and cook over medium heat for about 5 minutes, or until browned. Add the pasta and reserved cooking water and cook, stirring, for another 3–4 minutes. Add the leftover ragoût, the pecorino and basil and stir for another 2 minutes over the heat. Adjust the seasoning, sprinkle with the extra pecorino shavings and serve.

FEATHERED GAME

WILD DUCK PÂTÉ

Serves 4

Preparation time:
30 minutes

Cooking time:
1 hour, plus 1 hour cooling

Resting time:
at least 12 hours

- 300 g/11 oz duck legs, boned
- 100 g/3½ oz pork belly (side)
- 4 tablespoons Armagnac
- 2 eggs
- 20 g/¾ oz (about 1 tablespoon) fine salt
- 1 teaspoon freshly ground pepper
- 1 piece pork fat (fatback), cut into 3 pieces
- 200 g/7 oz fresh foie gras, cut into thick slices
- rocket (arugula) leaves, to serve

1.
Mince (grind) the duck and pork belly (side) in a mincer (grinder) and put into a large bowl. Add the Armagnac, eggs, salt and pepper and mix together with your hands until combined.

2.
Preheat the oven to 170°C/340°F/Gas Mark 3–4.

3.
Put a piece of the pork fat (fatback) into the bottom of a terrine dish or loaf pan, add a layer of the meat mixture, then top with half the foie gras slices and a piece of the pork fat. Cover with half the remaining meat mixture, the other half of the foie gras, then the rest of the meat mixture, pressing the layers down firmly. Top with the remaining piece of pork fat. Put the terrine into a large ovenproof dish and carefully pour hot water into the dish to come halfway up the sides of the terrine to create a bain-marie. Cook in the oven for 1 hour.

4.
When the pâté is cooked, remove from the oven and leave to cool for 1 hour at room temperature, then chill in the refrigerator for at least 12 hours before eating.

5.
Serve the pâté cut into slices with a rocket (arugula) salad.

WILD DUCK BREASTS WITH LIME AND CELERIAC PURÉE

Serves 4

Preparation time:
35 minutes

Cooking time:
40–50 minutes

- 1 celeriac (celery root), peeled and cut into chunks
- 6 tablespoons olive oil
- 3 organic limes
- 4 wild duck breasts, skin left on
- 50 g/2 oz (4 tablespoons) butter
- 4 tablespoons soy sauce
- ½ bunch coriander (cilantro), finely chopped
- salt and freshly ground pepper

1.

Steam the celeriac (celery root) in a steamer set over a saucepan of simmering water for 20–30 minutes until tender. Transfer the celeriac to a food processor with 2 tablespoons of the oil and process until it is a smooth purée. Season with salt and pepper, then cover and keep warm.

2.

Using a zester, remove the thin outer layer of zest from the limes. Blanch the lime zest for 5 minutes in a saucepan of boiling water, then drain and plunge into a bowl of cold water and drain again. Squeeze the juice from the limes and set aside.

3.

Season the duck breasts with salt and pepper. Heat the butter and the remaining oil in a frying pan or skillet over high heat, add the duck breasts, skin-side down, and cook for 5 minutes. Turn them over and cook for another 3 minutes. Remove the duck from the pan with a slotted spoon and put onto a plate, cover with aluminium foil and leave to rest.

4.

Add the lime zest and juice to the cooking liquid in the pan and simmer for 5 minutes to reduce the liquid. Pour in the soy sauce, bring to the boil, then remove from the heat.

5.

Carve the duck breasts into thick slices and arrange them on a serving plate. Coat them with the sauce, sprinkle over the coriander (cilantro) and serve with the celeriac purée.

DAUBE OF WILD DUCK

Serves 4

Preparation time:
35 minutes

Cooking time:
1 hour 10 minutes – 1 hour
20 minutes

- 2 wild ducks, plucked, gutted and cut into pieces
- 50 g/2 oz (4 tablespoons) butter
- 2 shallots, finely chopped
- 1 tablespoon plain (all-purpose) flour
- 1 sprig thyme
- 1 bay leaf
- 500 ml/17 fl oz (generous 2 cups) red wine
- 500 ml/17 fl oz (generous 2 cups) chicken stock (broth)
- salt and freshly ground pepper
- pan-fried pumpkin or cooked fresh pasta, to serve

1.
Season the duck pieces with salt and pepper. Melt the butter in a large flameproof casserole (Dutch oven) over medium-high heat until it starts foaming. Add the duck and shallots and cook for 5–10 minutes until coloured.

2.
Add the flour, thyme and bay leaf, then pour in the red wine and simmer for 5–10 minutes to reduce the liquid by half. Pour in the chicken stock (broth), reduce the heat to low and simmer for 1 hour.

3.
When the meat is cooked and meltingly tender, remove the bay leaf, adjust the seasoning, if necessary, and serve with pan-fried pumpkin or cooked fresh pasta.

WILD DUCK TERRINE WITH PISTACHIOS

Serves 4

Preparation time:
35 minutes

Cooking time:
1 hour, plus 1 hour cooling

Chilling time:
at least 12 hours

- 2 wild ducks, plucked, gutted and boned
- 300 g/11 oz pork belly (side)
- 2 eggs
- 4 tablespoons ruby port
- 20 g/¾ oz (about 1 tablespoon) salt
- 1 tablespoon freshly ground pepper
- 100 g/3½ oz (⅔ cup) pistachios, blanched
- 1 piece pork fat (fatback)
- 2 bay leaves

To serve:
- slices of toasted bread
- rocket (arugula)
- 12 cherries

1.
Remove the skin from the duck breasts (but reserve it), then cut the meat into pieces with a sharp knife. Mince (grind) the duck meat and pork belly (side) in a mincer (grinder) and put into a large bowl. Add the eggs, port, salt, pepper and pistachios and mix together with your hands until combined.

2.
Preheat the oven to 160°C/325°F/Gas Mark 3.

3.
Place the piece of pork fat (fatback) in the bottom of a terrine dish or loaf pan, add the meat mixture, pressing it down well, then lay the bay leaves and the reserved duck skin on top. Put the terrine into a large ovenproof dish and carefully pour hot water into the ovenproof dish to come halfway up the sides of the terrine to create a bain-marie. Cook in the oven for 1 hour.

4.
When the terrine is cooked, remove from the oven and leave to cool for 1 hour at room temperature, then chill in the refrigerator for at least 12 hours before eating.

5.
Serve the wild duck terrine on slices of toasted bread with rocket (arugula) and cherries on the side.

DUCK, APRICOT AND SAVORY PÂTÉ

Serves 4

Preparation time:
45 minutes

Cooking time:
45 minutes, plus 1 hour cooling

Chilling time:
at least 12 hours

- 3 wild ducks, plucked, gutted and boned
- 4 apricots, pitted and cut into small pieces
- 5 sprigs savory, rosemary or thyme, leaves removed from stalks and chopped
- 1 egg
- 2 teaspoons salt
- 1 teaspoon freshly ground pepper
- sprigs savory, to decorate (optional)

1.
Preheat the oven to 180°C/350°F/Gas Mark 4.

2.
Coarsely mince (grind) the meat in a mincer (grinder). Put into a large bowl, add the apricot pieces, herbs, egg, salt and pepper and mix together with your hands until thoroughly combined.

3.
Put the mixture into a terrine dish or loaf pan, pressing it down well. Put the terrine into a large ovenproof dish and carefully pour hot water into the dish to come halfway up the sides of the terrine to create a bain-marie. Cook in the oven for 45 minutes.

4.
When the pâté is cooked, remove from the oven, leave to cool for 1 hour at room temperature, then chill in the refrigerator for at least 12 hours before eating.

5.
Decorate the pâté with sprigs of savory, if using, before serving.

CROSS-BRED DUCK ROASTED WITH CHERRIES AND OLIVES

Serves 4

Preparation time:
20 minutes

Cooking time:
1 hour 10 minutes

- 1 cross-bred duck, plucked, gutted and trussed with kitchen string or twine
- 4 tablespoons olive oil
- 100 g/3½ oz (generous ¾ cup) black olives, pitted
- 4 tablespoons soy sauce
- 200 ml/7 fl oz (scant 1 cup) dessert wine
- 200 g/7 oz (1⅓ cups) cherries, pitted
- salt and freshly ground pepper
- Celeriac Purée (page 84), to serve

1.
Preheat the oven to 180°C/350°F/Gas Mark 4.

2.
Season the duck with salt and pepper. Heat the oil in a large flameproof casserole (Dutch oven) over high heat, add the duck and sear for 10 minutes, or until golden all over. Remove from the heat, cover and cook in the oven for 25 minutes.

3.
Lift the duck out of the casserole, remove the breasts with a very sharp knife and set them aside, cover and keep warm. Remove the legs, put them back into the casserole and add the olives, soy sauce and wine. Cover and cook in the oven for another 35 minutes.

4.
Remove the casserole from the oven, add the cherries and duck breasts and adjust the seasoning, if necessary. Serve immediately with celeriac purée.

TIP
Cooking the duck is done in two stages because the breasts cook more quickly than the legs. If you prefer, replace the cross-bred duck with two wild ducks.

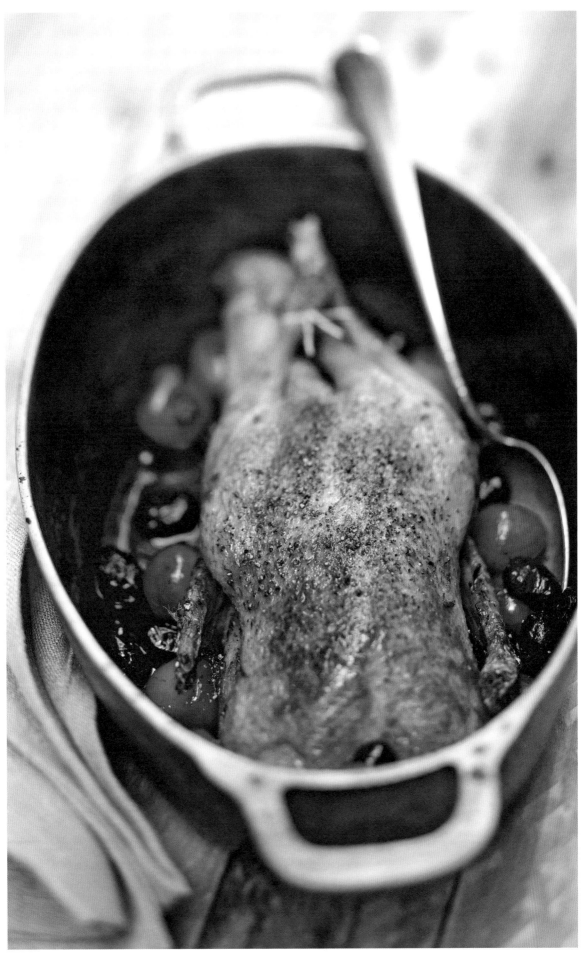

POTTED MALLARD DUCK AND TURNIP

Serves 4

Preparation time:
20 minutes

Cooking time:
20–25 minutes, plus cooling time

- 20 baby new season's turnips, peeled
- 3 tablespoons sunflower oil
- 40 g/1½ oz (3 tablespoons) butter
- 4 mallard ducks, plucked, gutted and cut into pieces
- 2 tablespoons clear (runny) honey
- 500 ml/17 fl oz (generous 2 cups) chicken stock (broth)
- salt

1.
Blanch the baby turnips for 5 minutes in a saucepan of boiling salted water. Drain and immediately plunge them into a bowl of cold water and drain again.

2.
Heat the oil and butter in a large frying pan or skillet over high heat, add the duck pieces and sear for 5–10 minutes until coloured on all sides. Add the honey and cook for another 5 minutes until caramelized. Add the turnips, then pour in the chicken stock (broth). Bring to the boil and turn off the heat.

3.
Transfer the duck pieces, turnips and stock to large sterilized preserving (canning) jars and seal them with airtight lids. Turn them upside down and leave to cool at room temperature.

TIP
You can store these jars in the refrigerator for 1–2 weeks.

FEATHERED GAME

MALLARD DUCKS WITH WILD THYME AND GREEN PEPPERCORNS

Serves 4

Preparation time:
10 minutes

Cooking time:
35 minutes

- 2 mallard ducks, plucked, gutted and cut into pieces
- 1 tablespoon sunflower oil
- 2 tablespoons soy sauce
- 50 g/2 oz (½ cup) green peppercorns in brine, drained
- 500 ml/17 fl oz (generous 2 cups) whipping or double (heavy) cream
- 10 sprigs wild thyme
- salt

1.
Season the duck pieces with salt. Heat the oil in a large flameproof casserole (Dutch oven) over high heat, add the duck pieces and sear for 5 minutes until coloured on all sides.

2.
Reduce the heat, add the soy sauce and deglaze the casserole by scraping the cooking juices off the bottom of the casserole with a wooden spoon or fish slice (spatula) and incorporate into the soy sauce. Simmer for 5 minutes to reduce the liquid.

3.
Add the green peppercorns and cream and simmer for about 25 minutes over low heat.

4.
Add the thyme sprigs to the casserole, stir to mix, then serve.

ROAST MALLARD DUCKS WITH PEAS AND BROAD BEANS

Serves 4

Preparation time:
40 minutes

Cooking time:
1 hour

- 300 g/11 oz broad (fava) beans in their pods, shelled (about 1 cup)
- 2 mallard ducks, plucked and gutted
- 4 tablespoons olive oil
- 50 g/2 oz (4 tablespoons) butter
- 2 rashers (slices) streaky (lean) bacon, cut into large lardons
- 100 ml/3½ fl oz (scant ½ cup) chicken stock (broth)
- 600 g/1 lb 5 oz peas in their pods, shelled (about 1¼ cup)
- I sprig thyme
- 2 bay leaves
- salt and freshly ground pepper

1.
Blanch the broad (fava) beans for 3 minutes in a saucepan of boiling water. Drain and immediately plunge the beans into a bowl of cold water and drain again, then slip off their skins and set aside.

2.
Preheat the oven to 180°C/350°F/Gas Mark 4.

3.
Season the ducks with salt and pepper. Heat the oil and butter in a large flameproof casserole (Dutch oven) over high heat, add the ducks and sear for 5–10 minutes until coloured on all sides. Add the bacon lardons, reduce the heat, pour in the chicken stock (broth), cover and cook in the oven for 20 minutes.

4.
Remove the casserole from the oven and add the peas, broad beans, thyme and bay leaves. Cover again and cook on the stove over low heat for 20 minutes, stirring frequently.

5.
Remove the cooked ducks from the casserole and carve them. Return the pieces to the casserole, adjust the seasoning, if necessary, and reheat for 10 minutes, or until hot, without putting the lid back on the casserole.

6.
Serve the duck, peas and broad beans straight from the casserole discarding the bay leaves.

PHEASANTS WITH WILD MUSHROOMS

Serves 4

Preparation time:
20 minutes

Cooking time:
1 hour 30 minutes

- 2 small pheasants, plucked and gutted
- 6 tablespoons olive oil
- 3 sprigs thyme
- 2 bay leaves
- 6 cloves pink garlic, unpeeled and crushed
- 1 kg/2¼ lb wild mushrooms
- 3 tablespoons red wine vinegar
- salt and freshly ground pepper
- mashed potatoes, to serve

1.

Season the pheasants with salt and pepper. Heat 2 tablespoons of the oil in a large flameproof casserole (Dutch oven) over high heat, add the pheasants and sear for 10 minutes, or until coloured all over. Add the thyme, bay leaves and crushed garlic, reduce the heat to low, cover and simmer for 45 minutes, turning the pheasants over occasionally.

2.

Add the mushrooms and remaining oil to the casserole and simmer for another 10 minutes. Add the vinegar and deglaze by scraping the cooking juices off the bottom of the casserole with a wooden spoon or fish slice (spatula) and incorporating them into the vinegar, then simmer for 5 minutes to reduce the liquid. Pour in 200 ml/7 fl oz (scant 1 cup) water, cover and simmer for another 20 minutes over very low heat.

3.

Adjust the seasoning, if necessary, discard the bay leaves and serve the pheasants with the mushrooms and some mashed potatoes on the side.

NOTE

The most common feathered game in France is pheasant, which has often been bred and released shortly before the beginning of the hunting season. This means the birds have less flavour than wild pheasant and do not need to be hung. The hen pheasant has finer flesh than the cock.

PHEASANT PÂTÉ WITH BLUEBERRIES

Serves 4

Preparation time:
25 minutes

Cooking time:
1 hour, plus 1 hour cooling

Chilling time:
at least 12 hours

- 2 pheasants, plucked, gutted and boned
- 300 g/11 oz pork belly (side)
- 150 g/5 oz (¾ cup) Puy (French green) lentils, cooked according to package instructions
- 200 g/7 oz (1⅓ cups) blueberries
- 1 egg
- 2 teaspoons salt
- 2 teaspoons freshly ground pepper
- 4 sprigs thyme

1.
Preheat the oven to 180°C/350°F/Gas Mark 4.

2.
Coarsely mince (grind) the pheasant meat and pork belly (side) through a mincer (grinder) and put into a large bowl. Add the lentils, blueberries, egg, salt and pepper and mix together with your hands until well combined.

3.
Spoon the mixture into individual ramekins, pressing it down firmly. Arrange the thyme sprigs on top. Put the ramekins in a large ovenproof dish and carefully pour hot water into the dish to come halfway up the sides of the ramekins to create a bain-marie. Cook in the oven for 1 hour.

4.
When the pâtés are cooked, remove from the oven and leave to cool for 1 hour at room temperature, then chill in the refrigerator for at least 12 hours before eating.

PHEASANT AND RED CABBAGE

Serves 4

Preparation time:
15 minutes

Cooking time:
1 hour 15 minutes – 1 hour
   25 minutes

- 1 large pheasant, plucked and gutted
- 4 tablespoons sunflower oil
- 70 g/2½ oz (5 tablespoons) butter
- 2 large onions, chopped
- 4 sprigs thyme
- 2 bay leaves
- 500 ml/17 fl oz (generous 2 cups) dry (hard) cider
- 1 small red cabbage, shredded on a mandoline or in a food processor
- salt and freshly ground pepper

1.

Season the pheasant with salt and pepper. Heat the oil in a large flameproof casserole (Dutch oven) over high heat, add the pheasant and sear for 5–10 minutes until coloured on all sides. Reduce the heat, add the butter, onions, thyme and bay leaves and cook for another 5 minutes until browned.

2.

Pour in the cider and simmer for 5–10 minutes, or until the liquid has reduced by three-quarters, then add the shredded cabbage and season with salt and pepper. Cover and simmer for 1 hour, stirring occasionally to prevent the cabbage sticking to the sides of the casserole.

3.

When the cabbage is very tender, remove from the heat. Take the pheasant out of the casserole and cut it into pieces. Put the pheasant pieces back into the casserole and serve at once.

FEATHERED GAME

PHEASANT AND PINE NUT PASTILLAS

Serves 4

Preparation time:
30 minutes

Cooking time:
1 hour 45 minutes, plus
   cooling time

- 2 tablespoons sunflower oil
- 130 g/4½ oz (1 stick plus
  1 tabespoon) butter,
  plus extra for greasing
- 2 pheasants, plucked, gutted
  and cut into pieces
- 3 large onions, finely chopped
- 4 tablespoons clear
  (runny) honey
- 1 teaspoon ground cinnamon
- 1 tablespoon curry powder
- 50 g/2 oz (scant ½ cup) pine nuts
- 16 sheets of filo (phyllo) or
  brik pastry
- salt and freshly ground pepper
- purslane, lamb's lettuce (corn
  salad) or dandelion leaves
  (greens), to serve

1.

Heat the oil and 50 g/2 oz (4 tablespoons) of the butter in a flameproof casserole (Dutch oven) over high heat, add the pheasants and sear for 5–10 minutes until coloured all over. Add the onions, honey and spices and cook for another 5 minutes, stirring frequently until caramelized. Season with salt and pepper, then pour in 200 ml/7 fl oz (scant 1 cup) water. Cover, reduce the heat to low and cook for 1 hour.

2.

Meanwhile, dry-fry the pine nuts in a non-stick frying pan or skillet over medium heat for 5 minutes, or until toasted. Remove from the heat and set aside.

3.

Once the pheasants are cooked, remove them from the casserole and leave to cool. Once cooled, take the meat off the bones by shredding it with 2 forks.

4.

Heat the softened onion mixture still in the casserole over high heat for 3 minutes, then transfer it to a large bowl and leave until just warm. Add the pheasant meat and toasted pine nuts and mix together. Adjust the seasoning, if necessary.

5.

Preheat the oven to 180°C/350°F/Gas Mark 4. Melt the remaining butter in a pan over low heat.

6.

Butter 4 small round pans, about 12 cm/4½ inches in diameter. Layer up 4 sheets of filo (phyllo) or brik pastry in each pan, brushing each layer with melted butter and letting the sheets hang over the sides of the pans. Spoon in the pheasant mixture and fold the filo sheets over the top of the filling. Lift the pans onto a large baking sheet. Brush the remaining butter over the pastillas. Turn them over so that the folded-over filo pastry rests on the baking sheet. Remove the pans and bake the pastillas in the oven for 20 minutes, or until golden and crisp. Serve hot with a salad of purslane, lamb's lettuce (corn salad) or dandelion leaves (greens).

PARTRIDGES ON TOASTED BREAD WITH VENTRÈCHE

Serves 4

Preparation time:
20 minutes

Cooking time:
55 minutes

- 4 thin slices ventrèche or pancetta, or pork belly (side)
- 4 young partridges, plucked and gutted
- 50 g/2 oz (4 tablespoons) butter
- 4 slices rustic bread
- 1 clove pink garlic, peeled
- salt and freshly ground pepper
- roast pumpkin, to serve

1.
Preheat the oven to 180°C/350°F/Gas Mark 4.

2.
Wrap the slices of ventrèche or pancetta, or pork belly (side) around the partridges and neatly secure with kitchen string or twine. Season them with salt and pepper.

3.
Heat the butter in a large flameproof casserole (Dutch oven) over high heat until it starts to foam. Add the partridges and sear for 5–10 minutes until coloured on all sides. Cover and cook in the oven for 45 minutes.

4.
Meanwhile, toast the bread slices, then rub them with the garlic and lay them on a serving platter.

5.
Remove the partridges from the casserole and arrange them on the toasted bread slices. Spoon over the cooking juices and serve with roast pumpkin.

NOTE
This way of preparing feathered game is a classic method in French gastronomy. Very simple, it is even better to eat this dish with your fingers.

PARTRIDGE ROASTED WITH STREAKY BACON AND HAY

Serves 4

Preparation time:
20 minutes

Cooking time:
1 hour

- 200 g/7 oz hay
- 1 large partridge, plucked, gutted and trussed with kitchen string or twine
- 2 rashers (slices) of streaky (standard) bacon
- 2 tablespoons sunflower oil
- 450 g/1 lb small Ratte (fingerling) potatoes
- 2 tablespoons hazelnut oil
- salt and freshly ground pepper

1.

Preheat the oven to 180°C/350°F/Gas Mark 4. Soak the hay in a basin of cold water.

2.

Season the partridge with salt and pepper. Lay the bacon rashers (slices) on top of the partridge and secure with kitchen string or twine.

3.

Heat the sunflower oil in a large flameproof casserole (Dutch oven) over high heat, add the partridge and sear for 10 minutes, or until coloured on all sides. Add the potatoes and cook for another 5 minutes until they are lightly coloured. Remove from the heat, add the damp hay, cover and cook in the oven for 45 minutes.

4.

When the partridge is cooked, remove the hay, scraping it off the skin of the partridge with a knife, then cut the partridge into 4 pieces. Arrange on a serving plate with the bacon and potatoes, drizzle over the hazelnut oil and serve.

ROAST PARTRIDGES WITH PUMPKIN AND HAZELNUT OIL

Serves 4

Preparation time:
15 minutes

Cooking time:
1 hour

- 4 young partridges, plucked and gutted
- 50 g/2 oz (4 tablespoons) butter, melted
- 50 ml/1¾ fl oz (scant ¼ cup) Cognac
- 800 g/1¾ lb pumpkin, de-seeded and sliced
- 2 tablespoons hazelnut oil
- 80 g/3 oz (½ cup) hazelnuts
- ½ bunch thyme
- salt and freshly ground pepper
- salad of dandelion leaves (greens), to serve

1.
Preheat the oven to 170°C/340°F/Gas Mark 3–4.

2.
Season the partridges with salt and pepper, then brush with the melted butter. Heat a large flameproof casserole (Dutch oven) over medium heat, add the partridges and sear for 5–10 minutes until coloured on all sides. Pour in the Cognac and set alight. Simmer for 5 minutes to reduce the cooking juices, basting the partridges frequently with them.

3.
Transfer the partridges to a large ovenproof dish. Arrange the pumpkin slices around them, spoon over the hazelnut oil and season with salt and pepper. Cook in the oven for 45 minutes, basting the partridges and the pumpkin frequently with the cooking juices.

4.
Place the partridges and pumpkin on a serving plate, sprinkle with the hazelnuts and thyme and serve with a dandelion salad.

TIP
Alternatively, you can sit the partridges on thick slices of bread before putting them into the oven if you like. That way the bread will catch all the juices.

STUFFED PARTRIDGE WITH KALE

Serves 2

Preparation time:
30 minutes

Cooking time:
1 hour 50 minutes

- 1 small brioche loaf, cut into small pieces
- 3 tablespoons milk
- 1 young partridge, plucked and gutted
- 200 g/7 oz fresh foie gras or chicken livers, cut into small dice
- 1 small head of kale
- 1 tablespoon sunflower oil
- 50 g/2 oz (4 tablespoons) butter
- 2 tablespoons clear (runny) honey
- 3 tablespoons white wine
- 2 thin rashers (slices) of smoked bacon, cut in half
- salt and freshly ground pepper

1.
Put the brioche pieces into a large bowl, pour in the milk to cover and leave to soak. Meanwhile, season the young partridge with salt and pepper.

2.
Add the foie gras or chicken livers to the bowl of soaked brioche, season with salt and pepper and mix together with your hands. Stuff the partridge with this mixture and close the bird by sewing up the cavity.

3.
Remove the outer kale leaves and set aside, then cut the kale heart into pieces and set aside as well.

4.
Heat the oil and butter in a large flameproof casserole (Dutch oven) over high heat, add the partridge and sear for 5–10 minutes until it is coloured on all sides. Add the honey and cook for 5 minutes until caramelized. Pour in the wine and simmer for about 5 minutes to reduce the liquid almost completely, basting the partridge several times with the cooking juices to lightly glaze it.

5.
Add the bacon and chopped kale heart to the bottom of the casserole, reduce the heat to low and cover the partridge with the outer kale leaves. Season with salt and pepper, cover and cook for 1 hour 30 minutes. Serve the partridge at the table directly from the casserole, carving it in front of your guests.

NOTE
The two most common types of partridge are the red partridge and the grey. The rock partridge, which is highly prized gastronomically, is experiencing a moderately rapid population reduction and is currently classified as near threatened by the International Union for Conservation of Nature.

WOOD PIGEON WITH BLACK TRUMPET MUSHROOMS

Serves 4

Preparation time:
20 minutes

Cooking time:
1 hour

- 4 wood pigeons, plucked and gutted
- 1 tablespoon goose or duck fat
- 1 large onion, finely chopped
- 2 bay leaves
- 1 teaspoon plain (all-purpose) flour
- 500 ml/17 fl oz (generous 2 cups) Cahors red wine
- 400 g/14 oz black trumpet mushrooms
- 4 slices cured ham, coarsely sliced
- salt and freshly ground pepper

1.

Split the wood pigeons in half and season with salt and pepper.

2.

Heat the goose or duck fat in a large flameproof casserole (Dutch oven) over high heat, add the pigeon halves and sear for about 10 minutes, or until coloured all over. Add the onion and bay leaves and cook for another 3 minutes until brown. Add the flour, mix well, then pour in the wine. Cover, reduce the heat to low and cook for 20 minutes.

3.

Add the mushrooms and ham to the casserole and cook for another 20 minutes. Adjust the seasoning, if necessary, and serve immediately.

WOOD PIGEON PÂTÉ WITH PISTACHIOS

Serves 4

Preparation time:
30 minutes

Cooking time:
1 hour 30 minutes, plus
   1 hour cooling

Chilling time:
at least 12 hours

- 5 wood pigeons, plucked, gutted and boned, meat cut into pieces
- 300 g/11 oz pork belly (side)
- 2 eggs
- 80 g/3 oz (½ cup) shelled pistachios
- 2 tablespoons Armagnac
- 20 g/2¾ oz (1 tablespoon) salt
- 1 tablespoon freshly ground pepper
- 1 piece pork fat (fatback), cut into strips
- 2 bay leaves

1.
Mince (grind) the pigeon meat and pork belly (side) in a mincer (grinder) and put into a large bowl. Add the eggs, pistachios, Armagnac, salt and pepper and mix together with your hands until thoroughly combined.

2.
Preheat the oven to 160°C/325°F/Gas Mark 3.

3.
Reserve 2 strips of the pork fat (fatback) and place the rest in the bottom of a terrine dish or loaf pan. Add the meat mixture, pressing it down firmly, then lay the bay leaves and reserved strips of pork fat on top. Put the terrine into a large ovenproof dish and carefully pour hot water into the dish to come halfway up the sides of the terrine to create a bain-marie. Cover with a double layer of aluminium foil and cook in the oven for 1 hour 30 minutes.

4.
When the pâté is cooked, remove from the oven and leave to cool for 1 hour at room temperature, then chill in the refrigerator for at least 12 hours before eating.

FEATHERED GAME

ROAST WOODCOCK ON TAPENADE CROUTES

Serves 4

Preparation time:
20 minutes

Cooking time:
35 minutes

- 70 g/2¾ oz (5 tablespoons) butter
- 8 green cabbage leaves, tough stalks removed, leaves coarsely chopped
- 4 woodcocks, plucked, gutted and trussed with kitchen string or twine, and their livers reserved
- 2 tablespoons tapenade
- 8 slices rustic bread
- 4 tablespoons sunflower oil
- salt and freshly ground pepper

1.
Preheat the oven to 180°C/350°F/Gas Mark 4.

2.
Heat the butter in a large frying pan or skillet until foaming. Add the chopped cabbage, season with salt and pepper and cook for 10 minutes over low heat, then remove from the heat. Set aside and keep warm.

3.
Blend the woodcock livers and tapenade together in a food processor until smooth, then spread the mixture on the slices of bread. Reduce the oven temperature to 160°C/325°F/Gas Mark 3. Put the bread on a baking sheet and cook in the oven for 20 minutes.

4.
Meanwhile, season the woodcock with salt and pepper. Heat the oil in a large flameproof casserole (Dutch oven) over high heat, add the woodcock and sear for 5–10 minutes until coloured on all sides. Pour in 100 ml/3 fl oz (scant ½ cup) water, reduce the heat slightly, cover and cook for 10 minutes.

5.
Arrange the cabbage on a serving platter, add the bread slices and top with the woodcocks. Serve at once.

TIP
Don't forget to provide your guests with finger bowls.

ROAST WOODCOCK WITH MIXED-BERRY SAUCE

Serves 4

Preparation time:
20 minutes

Cooking time:
45 minutes

- 4 woodcock, plucked
- 4 tablespoons sunflower oil
- 50 g/2 oz (4 tablespoons) butter
- 4 tablespoons balsamic
  vinegar
- 100 g/3½ oz (⅔ cup)
  blackberries
- 100 g/3½ oz (scant 1 cup)
  redcurrants, stalks removed
- 100 g/3½ oz (⅔ cup)
  blueberries
- 100 g/3½ oz (1 cup) cranberries
- salt and freshly ground pepper
- Celeriac Purée (page 84),
  to serve

1.
Gut the woodcock and return their livers and gizzards to the cavities. With kitchen string or twine, tie the wings against the bodies of the birds and tie the legs together. Season with salt and pepper.

2.
Heat the oil and butter in a large flameproof casserole (Dutch oven) over high heat, add the woodcock and sear for 5 minutes until coloured on all sides. Pour in the vinegar and deglaze the casserole by scraping the cooking juices off the bottom of the casserole with a wooden spoon or fish slice (spatula) and incorporating them into the vinegar. Simmer for 5 minutes to reduce the liquid. Pour in 400 ml/14 fl oz (1⅔ cups) water, reduce the heat to low, cover and cook for 20 minutes.

3.
When the woodcock are cooked, remove them from the casserole and put onto a large platter. Add the fruits to the casserole and heat through for 3 minutes, stirring gently. Adjust the seasoning, if necessary, then put the woodcock back into the sauce. Serve with celeriac purée.

QUAILS IN RED WINE SAUCE

Serves 4

Preparation time:
15 minutes

Cooking time:
1 hour 25 minutes

- 4 quails, plucked and gutted
- 100 g/3½ oz (7 tablespoons) butter
- 2 bay leaves
- 1 sprig thyme
- 2 rashers (slices) streaky (standard) bacon, cut into large lardons
- 200 g/7 oz small or baby (pearl) onions, peeled
- 750 ml/25 fl oz (3 cups) red wine
- 250 ml/8 fl oz (1 cup) veal stock (broth)
- salt and freshly ground pepper
- cooked fresh pasta, to serve

1.

Season the quails with salt and pepper. Heat the butter in a large flameproof casserole (Dutch oven) over high heat until foaming. Add the quails and sear for 5–10 minutes, or until coloured on all sides. Add the bay leaves, thyme, bacon lardons and onions and cook for 3 minutes until browned.

2.

Pour in the red wine and deglaze the pan by scraping the cooking juices off the bottom of the casserole with a wooden spoon or fish slice (spatula) and incorporating them into the wine. Simmer for 5 minutes to reduce the liquid by half. Pour in the veal stock (broth), reduce the heat to low and simmer, uncovered, for about 1 hour, basting the quails with the cooking juices occasionally.

3.

Serve the quails with cooked fresh pasta.

QUAIL RILLETES WITH RAISINS

Serves 4

Preparation time:
40 minutes

Cooking time:
1 hour 5 minutes

Resting time:
at least 12 hours

- 4 tablespoons goose or
  duck fat
- 6 quails, plucked, gutted and
  cut in half
- 2 cloves pink garlic, unpeeled
  and crushed
- 2 bay leaves
- 2 sprigs thyme
- 70 g/2¾ oz (½ cup) raisins or
  chopped dried apricot
- salt and freshly ground pepper
- slices of rustic bread,
  to serve

1.
Heat the goose or duck fat in a large flameproof casserole (Dutch oven) over very low heat, add the quail halves, garlic, bay leaves and thyme, cover and cook for 1 hour, stirring occasionally.

2.
Remove the quails from the casserole, leave to cool slightly, then pull the meat off the bones with your fingers and set aside.

3.
Drain the cooked garlic pulp from the casserole, reserving half the cooking juices. Discard the thyme, bay leaf and garlic skins.

4.
Finely chop the quail meat, leaving a few pieces intact. Mix the meat with the raisins or apricot and garlic pulp in a large bowl. Pour over the reserved cooking juices, season with salt and pepper and mix together until combined.

5.
Pack the quail rillettes into 1–2 sterilized preserving (canning) jars. Seal the jars with airtight lids and keep in the refrigerator for at least 12 hours.

6.
Before serving, let the quail rillettes come to room temperature. Eat them spread on slices of rustic bread.

TIP
You can store these jars in the refrigerator for 1–2 weeks.

FEATHERED GAME

QUAIL PÂTÉ WITH CHICKEN LIVERS

Serves 4

Preparation time:
25 minutes

Cooking time:
1 hour, plus 1 hour cooling

Chilling time:
at least 12 hours

- 6 quails, plucked, gutted and boned
- 100 g/3½ oz pork belly (side)
- 100 g/3½ oz chicken livers
- 1 egg
- 3 tablespoons Armagnac or Cognac
- 1¼ teaspoons salt
- 1 teaspoon freshly ground pepper
- 1 piece pork fat (fatback), cut into strips
- 2 sprigs thyme (optional)

1.
Preheat the oven to 180°C/350°F/Gas Mark 4.

2.
Coarsely mince (grind) the quail meat, pork belly (side) and chicken livers in a mincer (grinder) and put into a large bowl. Add the egg, Armagnac or Cognac, salt and pepper and mix together with your hands until combined.

3.
Put the meat mixture into a terrine or loaf pan, pressing it down firmly, then lay the strips of pork fat (fatback) and thyme sprigs, if using, on top. Place the terrine or loaf pan in a large ovenproof dish and carefully pour hot water into the dish to come halfway up the sides of the terrine or loaf pan to create a bain-marie. Cook in the oven for 1 hour.

4.
When the pâté is cooked, remove from the oven and leave to cool at room temperature for 1 hour, then chill in the refrigerator for at least 12 hours before eating.

QUAIL AND ONION COMPOTE

Serves 4

Preparation time:
30 minutes

Cooking time:
2 hours 25 minutes

- 2 tablespoons sunflower oil
- 4 onions, finely chopped
- 8 quails, plucked and gutted
- 750 ml/25 fl oz (3 cups)
  dessert wine
- salt and freshly ground pepper
- mashed potatoes, to serve

1.
Heat the oil in a large flameproof casserole (Dutch oven) over low heat, add the onions and cook for 10–15 minutes, or until caramelized. Add the quails, then pour in the wine and cook, uncovered, for 2 hours over very low heat.

2.
When the quails are tender, remove the casserole from the heat, transfer the quails to a plate with a slotted spoon and leave to cool a little.

3.
When the quails are cool enough to handle, remove the bones and shred the meat using 2 forks.

3.
Put the casserole back over a medium heat and simmer for about 5 minutes to reduce the cooking juices until they thicken slightly. Season with salt and pepper and return the meat to the casserole. Serve immediately with mashed potatoes.

QUAIL AND MUSHROOM FRICASSEE

Preparation time:
30 minutes

Cooking time:
20–25 minutes

- 8 quails, plucked, gutted and cut into 4 pieces each
- 70 g/2¾ oz (5 tablespoons) butter
- 1 tablespoon sunflower oil
- 200 g/7 oz golden chanterelle mushrooms, halved, if large
- 200 g/7 oz chanterelle mushrooms, halved, if large
- 200 g/7 oz ceps (porcini), halved, if large
- 200 g/7 oz black trumpet mushrooms, halved, if large
- 2 shallots, chopped
- salt and freshly ground pepper
- chives, snipped, to sprinkle
- Pan-fried Chestnuts (page 30), to serve

1.
Season the quail pieces with salt and pepper. Heat the butter and oil in a large frying pan or skillet over high heat, add the quail pieces and sear for 5 minutes, or until coloured on one side, then turn them over and reduce the heat. (This may need to be done in batches, depending on the size of the pan.) Add the mushrooms and shallots and cook for 10–15 minutes, stirring frequently.

2.
Sprinkle with snipped chives and serve with pan-fried chestnuts.

BLANQUETTE OF QUAIL AND BLACK TRUMPET MUSHROOMS

Serves 4–6

Preparation time:
30 minutes

Cooking time:
1 hour 40 minutes

- 1 large onion
- 1 clove
- 4 quails, plucked, gutted and cut into 4 pieces each
- 1 carrot
- 1 leek
- 100 g/3½ oz (7 tablespoons) butter
- 500 g/1 lb 2 oz black trumpet mushrooms
- 50 g/2 oz (scant ½ cup) plain (all-purpose) flour
- 200 ml/7 fl oz (scant 1 cup) whipping or double (heavy) cream
- salt and freshly ground pepper
- cooked rice, to serve

1.
Stud the onion with the clove. Put it in a large casserole (Dutch oven) with the quail pieces and the whole carrot and leek. Cover with enough water to come 5 cm/2 inches above the ingredients and bring to the boil over high heat. Reduce the heat to low and cook for 1 hour.

2.
Heat 50 g/2 oz (4 tablespoons) of the butter in a frying pan or skillet over high heat, add the mushrooms and fry for 5 minutes, stirring constantly.

3.
When the quail pieces are cooked, remove from the casserole with the vegetables and put onto a large plate. Keep warm. Reserve the cooking liquid that is still in the casserole.

4.
Melt the remaining butter in another large casserole over medium heat, add the flour and stir in to make a roux. Remove from the heat and pour the reserved cooking liquid over the roux. Whisk until the sauce thickens. Add the cream, the quail pieces, vegetables and mushrooms with their cooking juices, then season with salt and pepper and heat for 10 minutes over very low heat, stirring frequently until piping hot.

5.
Serve immediately with cooked rice.

MUSHROOMS, HERBS & SNAILS

POTTED CEPS

Serves 4

Preparation time:
20 minutes

Sterilizing time:
2 hours

- 1.5 kg/3¼ lb small, very fresh ceps (porcini), cut in half or into 3 pieces if very large
- 2 bay leaves
- 2 sprigs thyme
- olive oil, to cover

1.
Blanch the ceps (porcini) for 1 minute in a large saucepan of boiling water, then drain.

2.
Pack the ceps into sterilized preserving (canning) jars, then add the bay leaves and thyme. Fill each jar with olive oil then seal the jars with tight-fitting lids and sterilise them in a pressure canner for 2 hours, or according to manufacturer's instructions (see note, below).

NOTE
When preserving wild produce, it is important to invest in a dedicated appliance called a canner – either a boiling-water canner or a pressure canner – which is a closed container with a lid, designed for sterilizing homemade preserves. Bacteria are generally killed when exposed to a wet heat between 80 and 100°C/176 and 212°F for an extended period, but spores, such as the ones causing botulism, are extremely tenacious. Therefore the higher temperatures (at least 116°C/240.8°F) achieved by a pressure canner are required for low-acid foods (meats, poultry, seafood, all fresh vegetables). Acid foods may be processed in either type of canner, but the boiling-water canner is generally deemed a better option since the process is faster and more economical. In the US, the National Center for Home Food Preservation provides detailed information on preserving a variety of produce.

PAN-FRIED CEPS AND FOIE GRAS

Serves 4

Preparation time:
20 minutes

Cooking time:
10–15 minutes

- 2 tablespoons olive oil
- 6 large ceps (porcini), cut into thick slices
- 3 cloves garlic, chopped
- 2 sprigs thyme
- 4 thick slices fresh foie gras
- 2 tablespoons balsamic vinegar
- salt and freshly ground pepper
- slices of toasted brioche, to serve

1.
Heat the oil in a large frying pan or skillet over high heat, add the ceps (porcini) and fry for 5 minutes until coloured. Add the garlic and thyme and fry for 2–3 minutes, stirring constantly, until browned. Season with salt and pepper, then divide the ceps among 4 plates.

2.
Return the pan over high heat, add the foie gras and sear for 1 minute on each side in the red-hot pan, without adding any fat. Season and place a slice on top of the ceps.

3.
Drizzle with a little balsamic vinegar and serve immediately with slices of toasted brioche.

TAGLIATELLE WITH CEPS

Serves 4

Preparation time:
15 minutes

Cooking time:
25 minutes

- 400 g/14 oz tagliatelle
- 4 tablespoons olive oil
- 1 kg/2¼ lb ceps (porcini),
  cut into large slices
- 4 cloves pink garlic, chopped
- 2 sprigs immature rosemary,
  needles only
- 4 tablespoons grated
  Parmesan cheese
- salt and freshly ground pepper

1.
Cook the pasta in a large saucepan of boiling salted water for 10–12 minutes, or according to package directions, until al dente. Drain, reserving a little of the cooking water.

2.
Heat the olive oil in a sauté pan over high heat, add the ceps (porcini) and sauté for 4–5 minutes, or until evenly coloured. Add the garlic and rosemary needles and season to taste. Cook, stirring, for another 5 minutes. Tip in the pasta, add a little of the reserved cooking water and heat through for 2 minutes.

3.
Sprinkle with the grated Parmesan and serve.

VEAL ESCALOPES WITH WALNUT CREAM AND SPRING CEPS

Serves 4

Preparation time:
20 minutes

Cooking time:
30 minutes

- 4 veal escalopes (scallops)
- 50 g/2 oz (4 tablespoons) butter
- 300 g/11 oz small spring ceps (porcini), sliced
- 50 ml/1¾ fl oz (scant ¼ cup) walnut wine
- 250 ml/8 fl oz (1 cup) whipping or double (heavy) cream
- 1 tablespoon walnut oil
- 1 sprig savory or thyme
- salt and freshly ground pepper
- cooked fresh tagliatelle, to serve

1.
Season the escalopes (scallops) with salt and pepper.

2.
Melt the butter in a frying pan or skillet until foaming. Add the escalopes and sear for 3 minutes, then add the ceps (porcini). Pour the wine into the pan and deglaze by scraping the cooking juices off the bottom of the pan with a wooden spoon or fish slice (spatula) and incorporate them into the wine. Simmer for 5 minutes to reduce the liquid by half. Pour in the cream and cook for another 15 minutes, basting the escalopes frequently with the sauce.

3.
Remove the escalopes and ceps from the pan with a slotted spoon and place on a serving plate. Whisk the oil into the sauce, then spoon it over the escalopes. Sprinkle with the savory or thyme and serve with cooked fresh tagliatelle.

CHANTERELLE AND CHESTNUT FRICASSEE

Serves 4

Preparation time:
20 minutes

Cooking time:
15 minutes

- 80 g/3 oz (6 tablespoons) butter
- 3 shallots, chopped
- 24 chestnuts, peeled, pre-cooked and cut into pieces
- 400 g/14 oz chanterelle mushrooms
- 1 bunch flowering garlic chives, snipped into short lengths, 2 scapes left whole, to garnish
- salt and freshly ground pepper

1.
Melt the butter in a large frying pan or skillet over medium heat until foaming. Add the shallots and fry for 2 minutes without letting them colour. Add the chestnut pieces and cook for about 5 minutes, or until browned. Add the chanterelles and fry for another 3 minutes, stirring constantly, over high heat. Season with salt and pepper, then remove from the heat.

2.
Sprinkle over the snipped garlic chives, garnish with the 2 scapes and serve immediately.

TIP
If you have fresh chestnuts, prepare them yourself following the instructions on page 30.

ROAST VEAL WITH FRICASSEE OF CHANTERELLE MUSHROOMS

Serves 4–6

Preparation time:
25 minutes

Cooking time:
1 hour 10 minutes

- 1 × 1.5-kg/3¼-lb veal roasting joint, off the bone, tied up with kitchen string or twine
- 4 tablespoons sunflower oil
- 80 g/3 oz (6 tablespoons) butter
- 100 ml/3½ fl oz (scant ½ cup) veal stock (broth)
- 4 shallots, chopped
- 1.5 kg/3¼ lb chanterelle mushrooms
- 1 bunch chives, chopped
- salt and freshly ground pepper

1.

Season the veal joint with salt and pepper. Heat the oil and half the butter in a large flameproof casserole (Dutch oven) over high heat, add the veal and sear for 5 minutes, or until coloured on all sides. Pour in the stock (broth) and deglaze by scraping the cooking juices off the bottom of the casserole with a wooden spoon or fish slice (spatula) and incorporate them into the stock. Simmer for 5 minutes to reduce the liquid. Reduce the heat to low and cook for 40 minutes, basting the veal frequently with the cooking juices.

2.

Melt the remaining butter in a large frying pan or skillet over medium heat until foaming, add the shallots and fry for 3 minutes without letting them colour. Add the mushrooms, increase the heat to high and sauté for 5 minutes. Season with salt and pepper, add the chives and stir until mixed in. Remove the pan from the heat.

3.

Remove the veal from the casserole and place onto a board. Increase the heat under the casserole and simmer for 5 minutes to reduce the cooking juices.

4.

Carve the veal into thick slices. Divide the fricasse of chanterelle mushrooms among serving plates, then arrange the veal on top. Coat with the hot cooking juices and serve.

GOLDEN CHANTERELLE AND HAZELNUT FRICASSEE

Serves 4

Preparation time:
20 minutes

Cooking time:
15 minutes

- 50 g/2 oz (4 tablespoons) butter
- 2 small shallots, chopped
- 500 g/1 lb 2 oz golden chanterelle mushrooms
- ½ bunch chives, snipped into small pieces
- 100 g/3½ oz (⅔ cup) dried hazelnuts, coarsely crushed
- 2 tablespoons hazelnut oil
- salt and freshly ground pepper
- roast game bird, to serve (optional)

1.
Melt the butter in a large frying pan or skillet over low-medium heat until foaming. Add the shallots and cook for 5 minutes, or until soft but not coloured. Add the mushrooms and cook for another 6–8 minutes, stirring, over high heat.

2.
Add the chives, crushed hazelnuts and hazelnut oil. Season with salt and pepper and mix everything together well. Serve the fricassee as a starter (appetizer) or as an accompaniment to a roast game bird.

NOTE
Golden chanterelles must be cleaned with a brush to remove any earth (soil) lodged in the pleats of their caps. If there is too much earth to brush away, rinse them quickly under cold running water in a colander and carefully dry the mushrooms with a clean cloth. Do not gather young golden chanterelles that are shaped like big office drawing (push) pins because they can be confused with poisonous mushrooms. See A Note on Mushrooms (page 239).

THIN GOLDEN CHANTERELLE MUSHROOM AND PARMESAN TART

Serves 4

Preparation time:
25 minutes

Cooking time:
30 minutes

- 4 tablespoons olive oil
- 500 g/1 lb 2 oz golden chanterelle mushrooms
- 2 shallots, chopped
- 1 sheet ready-rolled all-butter puff pastry
- 50 g/2 oz Parmesan cheese, grated
- 1 bunch chives, chopped (optional)
- salt and freshly ground pepper
- salad, to serve

1.
Preheat the oven to 180°C/350°F/Gas Mark 4.

2.
Heat the oil in a large frying pan or skillet over high heat, add the mushrooms and shallots and cook for 1 minute. Remove the pan from the heat.

3.
Unroll the puff pastry dough onto a baking sheet lined with baking parchment and fold up the edges to give a rectangular shape. Prick the bottom of the pastry with a fork. Spread the mushrooms over the pastry, drizzle with the oil remaining in the pan and sprinkle with the Parmesan. Bake in the oven for 25 minutes, or until the pastry is golden and the cheese has melted. Remove from the oven and sprinkle with the chopped chives, if using. Serve the tart warm or cold with a salad.

WARM SALAD OF LENTILS, GOLDEN CHANTERELLE MUSHROOMS AND CRISPY SHALLOTS

Serves 4

Preparation time:
20 minutes

Cooking time:
35 minutes

- 300 g/11 oz (1½ cups) Puy (French green) lentils
- 3 large shallots, chopped
- 2 tablespoons plain (all-purpose) flour
- 3 tablespoons olive oil
- 400 g/14 oz golden chanterelle mushrooms
- 4 tablespoons walnut oil
- 4 tablespoons sherry vinegar
- a few sprigs chervil, leaves only
- salt and freshly ground pepper

1.
Put the lentils into a large saucepan and pour in enough water to cover. Bring to the boil, then reduce the heat and cook for 20 minutes, or until tender. When they are cooked, leave the lentils in the cooking water so that they become very soft.

2.
Dust the chopped shallots with the flour.

3.
Heat 1 tablespoon of the olive oil in a small frying pan or skillet over medium heat, add the shallots and fry for 5 minutes until they are a rich golden colour. Turn off the heat and leave the shallots in the pan.

4.
Heat the remaining olive oil in a large frying pan or skillet over high heat, add the mushrooms and cook for 5 minutes. Drain the lentils, add them to the pan, then pour in the walnut oil and sherry vinegar. Heat through, stirring, for 3–4 minutes.

5.
Season the lentil mixture with salt and pepper and add the chervil and crispy shallots. Mix well and serve warm.

MUSHROOMS, HERBS & SNAILS

SALAD OF PIED BLEU MUSHROOMS WITH BAY LEAVES AND THYME

Serves 4

Preparation time:
15 minutes

Cooking time:
35 minutes

- 7 tablespoons olive oil
- 400 g/14 oz pied bleu mushrooms
- 8 small cloves pink garlic, unpeeled and crushed
- 4 sprigs thyme
- 4 bay leaves
- 150 ml/5 fl oz (⅔ cup) good-quality red wine vinegar
- salt and freshly ground pepper
- steak or veal escalope (scallop), to serve (optional)
- mixed fresh herbs, to garnish

1.
Heat 5 tablespoons of the oil in a large frying pan or skillet over high heat, add the mushrooms and garlic and fry for 5 minutes, or until coloured. Reduce the heat to low, season with salt and pepper, add the thyme and bay leaves and cook for 25 minutes.

2.
Pour in the vinegar and deglaze by scraping the cooking juices off the bottom of the pan with a wooden spoon or fish slice (spatula) and incorporate them into the vinegar. Simmer for 3 minutes, stirring, to reduce the liquid. Turn off the heat under the pan and add the remaining 2 tablespoons oil. Season with salt and pepper.

3.
Serve the salad warm or cold, as a starter (appetizer) or as an accompaniment to steak or a veal escalope (scallop).

VARIATION
This recipe also tastes delicious when it is made using ceps (porcini) or milk cap mushrooms.

FRICASSEE OF FAIRY RING MUSHROOMS AND CRAYFISH WITH BASIL

Serves 4

Preparation time:
30 minutes

Cooking time:
55 minutes

- 1 kg/2¼ lb crayfish
- 4 tablespoons olive oil
- 1 teaspoon tomato purée (paste)
- 200 ml/7 fl oz (scant 1 cup) white wine
- 500 ml/17 fl oz (generous 2 cups) whipping or double (heavy) cream
- 1 sprig thyme
- 1 bay leaf
- 50 g/2 oz (4 tablespoons) butter
- 400 g/14 oz fairy ring mushrooms
- 1 handful of basil leaves
- salt and freshly ground pepper

1.
Blanch the crayfish for 3 minutes in a large saucepan of boiling water. Drain, remove and reserve the meat and crush the shells.

2.
Heat the oil in a large flameproof casserole (Dutch oven) over high heat, add the crushed crayfish shells and tomato purée (paste), then pour in the white wine and cook for 5–10 minutes or until the liquid has reduced by three-quarters. Add the cream, thyme and bay leaf, reduce the heat to low and simmer for 30 minutes.

3.
Remove the bay leaf and thyme from the casserole. Pass the mixture first through a vegetable mill or mouli, then through a fine sieve (strainer) into a pan. Season with salt and pepper. To keep the sauce hot, put the pan into a large ovenproof dish and carefully pour hot water into the dish to come halfway up the sides of the pan to create a bain-marie.

4.
Melt the butter in a large frying pan or skillet over low heat until foaming. Add the crayfish meat and cook for 5 minutes. Add the mushrooms, season with salt and pepper and cook, stirring, for another 5 minutes.

5.
Add the hot sauce and basil leaves to the pan, mix well and serve immediately.

MOREL-MUSHROOM FRICASSEE WITH WILD ASPARAGUS

Serves 4

Preparation time:
10 minutes

Cooking time:
15 minutes

- 80 g/3 oz (6 tablespoons) butter
- 2 small shallots, chopped
- 400 g/14 oz morel mushrooms
- 150 ml/5 fl oz (⅔ cup) vin jaune
- 200 g/7 oz wild asparagus
- 1 tablespoon thick crème fraîche
- salt and freshly ground pepper

1.

Melt the butter in a large flameproof casserole (Dutch oven) over low heat until foaming. Add the shallots and fry for 3 minutes until meltingly soft, but not coloured.

2.

Add the morel mushrooms, pour in the wine and simmer for 5–10 minutes, stirring, until the liquid has reduced by three quarters. Add the wild asparagus and crème fraîche, bring to the boil and cook for 1 minute, then turn off the heat.

3.

Season with salt and pepper and serve.

NOTE

The morel is a springtime mushroom that is full of flavour, but rare. Its conical cap is pitted with a honeycomb of small deep holes so it is essential to clean it carefully in several changes of water. Dark-capped morels, that are brownish-black in colour, are the most sought after, while 'blonde' morels are less rare. It is essential to ensure they are fully cooked to remove the toxic substances they contain.

RUMP STEAKS AND MORELS WITH CREAM

Serves 4

Preparation time:
15 minutes

Cooking time:
25 minutes

- 4 rump (sirloin) steaks
- 50 g/2 oz (4 tablespoons) butter
- 1 tablespoon sunflower oil
- 50 ml/1¾ fl oz (scant ¼ cup) veal stock (broth)
- 180 g/6¼ oz fresh morel mushrooms
- 500 ml/17 fl oz (generous 2 cups) whipping or double (heavy) cream
- salt and freshly ground pepper
- cooked fresh tagliatelle, to serve

1.
Season the steaks with salt and pepper. Heat the butter and oil in a large frying pan or skillet over medium heat until the butter is foaming. Add the steaks and sear for 3–4 minutes on each side, until cooked and coloured according to personal taste. Transfer the steaks to a plate and set aside.

2.
Pour in the veal stock (broth) and deglaze the pan by scraping the cooking juices off the bottom of the pan with a wooden spoon or fish slice (spatula) and incorporate them into the stock. Simmer for 5 minutes, or until almost all the liquid has evaporated. Add the morels and cream and cook, stirring, for another 5 minutes. Add the steaks and serve with cooked fresh tagliatelle.

VARIATION
If you use dried morels, put 80 g/3 oz in a large bowl, cover them with warm water and leave to soak for about 30 minutes. Drain the mushrooms and dry with paper towels. Strain the soaking water and set it aside. Cook the steaks according to the recipe above, but deglaze the pan with the reserved soaking water and let it reduce by three-quarters. Add the rehydrated morels and the cream and bring to the boil. Season with salt and pepper, then cook for 5 minutes over high heat before putting the steaks into the sauce.

FRICASSEE OF BLACK TRUMPET MUSHROOMS AND GIZZARDS

Serves 4

Preparation time:
15 minutes

Cooking time:
10 minutes

- 300 g/11 oz (2¾ sticks) butter
- 800 g/1¾ lb black trumpet mushrooms
- 300 g/11 oz preserved duck gizzards, halved
- 6 sprigs flat-leaf parsley, coarsely chopped
- salt and freshly ground pepper
- toasted rustic bread, to serve

1.
Heat the butter in a large frying pan or skillet over medium heat until foaming. Add the mushrooms and gizzards and cook for 5 minutes. Remove from the heat. Season with salt and pepper and add the parsley.

2.
Transfer the fricassee to 4 serving plates and serve with toasted rustic bread.

MASHED POTATOES WITH BLACK TRUMPET MUSHROOMS AND HAZELNUT OIL

Serves 4

Preparation time:
30 minutes

Cooking time:
35 minutes

- 500 g/1 lb 2 oz potatoes (Bintje or another variety suitable for mashing), peeled
- 150 ml/5 fl oz (⅔ cup) milk
- 80 g/3 oz (6 tablespoons) butter
- 2 tablespoons hazelnut oil
- 200 g/7 oz black trumpet mushrooms
- salt and freshly ground pepper
- sausages or roast pork, to serve

1.
Cook the potatoes in a large saucepan of boiling salted water for 20 minutes, or until tender.

2.
Meanwhile, heat the milk in another saucepan until it comes to the boil. When the potatoes are cooked, drain them, reserving a little of their cooking water and return them to the pan. Using a potato masher, mash with a little of the reserved cooking water and the boiling milk, then season with salt and pepper. Mix in 50 g/2 oz (4 tablespoons) of the butter, then stir in the hazelnut oil and keep hot.

3.
Melt the remaining butter in a frying pan or skillet over medium heat until foaming. Add the mushrooms and cook, stirring, for 5 minutes, then remove from the heat and coarsely chop.

4.
Add the mushrooms to the mashed potatoes and serve as an accompaniment to sausages or roast pork.

CREAM OF MILK CAP MUSHROOM SOUP WITH PAN-FRIED FAIRY RING MUSHROOMS

Serves 4

Preparation time:
25 minutes

Cooking time:
45–50 minutes

- 100 g/3½ oz (7 tablespoons) butter
- 700 g/1 lb 8½ oz milk cap mushrooms, chopped
- 200 g/7 oz button mushrooms, chopped
- 200 ml/7 fl oz (scant 1 cup) chicken stock (broth)
- 500 ml/17 fl oz (generous 2 cups) whipping or double (heavy) cream
- 200 g/7 oz fairy ring mushrooms, chopped
- 2 tablespoons hazelnut oil
- salt and freshly ground pepper

1.
Heat 80 g/3 oz (6 tablespoons) of the butter in a large flameproof casserole (Dutch oven) over medium heat, add the milk cap mushrooms and button mushrooms and cook for 5 minutes. Pour in the chicken stock (broth) and simmer for 5–10 minutes to reduce the liquid by half. Pour in the cream, reduce the heat and simmer for 30 minutes over low heat, stirring occasionally.

2.
Transfer the mixture to a blender or food processor and process until it is a smooth, creamy consistency. Season with salt and pepper and keep hot.

3.
Melt the remaining butter in a frying pan or skillet over medium heat, add the fairy ring mushrooms and cook for 2 minutes. Remove from the heat.

4.
Pour the blended mixture into 4 serving bowls, spoon the fried fairy ring mushrooms on top and drizzle each serving with hazelnut oil. Serve.

WILD MUSHROOM AND HERB LOAF

Serves 4

Preparation time:
30 minutes

Cooking time:
55 minutes

- 50 g/2 oz (4 tablespoons) butter, plus extra for greasing
- 400 g/14 oz mixed wild mushrooms (black trumpet, golden chanterelles, fairy ring, ceps [porcini], and hedgehog mushrooms)
- ½ bunch chives, chopped
- ½ bunch flat-leaf parsley, chopped
- 100 g/3½ oz (scant 1 cup) plain (all-purpose) flour
- 2 teaspoons baking powder
- 3 eggs, beaten
- 100 ml/3½ fl oz (scant ½ cup) milk
- 5 tablespoons olive oil
- 100 g/3½ oz (scant 1 cup) grated Gruyère cheese
- salt and freshly ground pepper
- salad, to serve

1.
Melt the butter in a large frying pan or skillet over medium heat until foaming. Add the mushrooms and cook for 5 minutes, stirring occasionally. Sprinkle over the herbs, then remove the pan from the heat. Season with salt and pepper.

2.
Preheat the oven to 170°C/340°F/Gas Mark 3–4 and butter a loaf pan.

3.
In a large bowl, combine the flour and baking powder.

4.
In another large bowl, mix together the eggs, milk and oil. Add the mushrooms (and their cooking liquid) and the grated Gruyère cheese and mix until combined. Pour into the bowl of flour and baking powder and mix until just combined into a smooth batter.

5.
Pour the batter into the prepared loaf pan, smooth the top level, and bake in the oven for 45 minutes, or until set. Once set, the centre of the loaf will not wobble when shaken.

6.
Turn out the loaf while it is hot and serve hot or cold with a salad.

WILD MUSHROOM PIZZA

Serves 4

Preparation time:
25 minutes

Drying time:
12 hours

Cooking time:
20–30 minutes

- 2 ceps (porcini), sliced
- 150 g/5 oz golden chanterelle mushrooms, halved if large
- 150 g/5 oz chanterelle mushrooms
- 150 g/5 oz pied bleu mushrooms
- 150 g/5 oz fairy ring mushrooms
- 1 x 260 g/ 9¼ oz ready-made pizza base (crust)
- 2 tablespoons single (light) cream
- 4 tablespoons olive oil
- 3 sprigs flat-leaf parsley, chopped
- ½ bunch chervil, chopped
- salt and freshly ground pepper
- salad, to serve

1.
The day before baking the pizza, spread out all the different mushrooms on a large platter and leave them to dry at room temperature overnight.

2.
The next day, preheat the oven to 230°C/450°F/Gas Mark 8 and line a baking sheet with baking parchment.

3.
Lay the pizza base (crust) on the prepared baking sheet and brush with the single (light) cream. Arrange the mushrooms attractively on top, season with salt and pepper and drizzle with half the oil. Bake the pizza in the oven for 20–30 minutes, until golden brown around the edges.

4.
Remove the cooked pizza from the oven and leave to cool slightly. Sprinkle over the herbs and drizzle with the remaining oil. Serve the pizza, hot or cold, with a salad.

FRIED RICE WITH SNAILS, BASIL AND WILD GARLIC

Serves 4

Preparation time:
10 minutes, plus snail
   preparation

Cooking time:
25 minutes

- 6 tablespoons olive oil
- 24 snails, prepared (see note)
- 3 cloves wild garlic, chopped
- 300 g/11 oz (1¾ cups) cooked
  white long-grain rice
- 6 tablespoons soy sauce
- 15 sprigs basil, torn
- salt and freshly ground pepper

1.
Heat the oil in a large frying pan or skillet over medium heat, add the snails and garlic and cook for 5 minutes, or until browned. Add the rice and soy sauce and stir to mix. Reduce the heat and cook for about 20 minutes, stirring occasionally.

2.
When the rice begins to colour, turn off the heat and transfer the rice with the snails to a serving plate. Season with salt and pepper and sprinkle over the basil. Serve very hot.

NOTE
When preparing snails for eating, don't cut corners. First of all, it's necessary to starve them for 10–12 days to purge them of any toxins. To do that, put the snails in an airy wooden box on a bed of grass, changing it every day. After 10–12 days, rinse the snails under cold running water, rubbing them thoroughly, then put them into a covered container containing 100 g/3½ oz (½ cup) coarse (kosher) salt, 100 ml/3½ fl oz (scant ½ cup) vinegar and 100 g/3½ oz (generous ¾ cup) plain (all-purpose) flour and leave for 2–3 hours in the refrigerator. Rinse them again, then plunge them into a large pan of boiling water and cook for 30 minutes. Remove the snails with a slotted spoon. Use a cocktail stick or toothpick to remove the snail flesh from the shells and return the snail flesh to the pan for another 30 minutes. Remove the pan from the heat and leave the snails to cool, then remove the black parts and rinse them again in cold water.

MUSHROOMS, HERBS & SNAILS

SNAIL AND WILD GARLIC PESTO VOL-AU-VENTS

Serves 4

Preparation time:
30 minutes, plus snail
   preparation

Cooking time:
1 hour 5 minutes

- 24 snails, prepared (page 174)
- 1 sprig thyme
- 1 bay leaf
- 1 carrot
- 1 large onion
- 24 individual mini vol-au-vent cases, baked
- salad, to serve

For the pesto:
- 8 leaves wild garlic
- 60 g/2¼ oz Parmesan cheese
- 3 tablespoons olive oil

1.
Put the snails into a saucepan of water and add the thyme, bay leaf, carrot and onion. Bring to the boil, then reduce the heat to low and simmer gently for 45 minutes. Turn off the heat and leave the snails to cool in their cooking water.

2.
Meanwhile, prepare the pesto. Blanch the wild garlic leaves for 2 minutes in a saucepan of boiling water. Drain and rinse under cold running water and drain again. Transfer them to a food processor, add the Parmesan and process, adding the olive oil in a thin steady stream so it is incorporated evenly until the desired consistency is reached.

3.
Preheat the oven to 180°C/350°F/Gas Mark 4.

4.
Arrange the vol-au-vent cases on a large baking sheet. Drain the snails, mix them with the pesto and spoon into the mini vol-au-vent cases, making sure to place 1 snail in each case. Cook in the oven for 10 minutes. Serve hot with a salad.

NOTE
Wild garlic grows abundantly in warm, shady places such as forests and meadows but also close to streams.

SNAILS WITH TOMATO AND MOUNTAIN HAM

Serves 4

Preparation time:
15 minutes, plus snail
   preparation

Cooking time:
50 minutes, plus cooling time

- 5 tablespoons olive oil
- 4 slices mountain ham (such
  as Serrano), not too thin, cut
  into pieces
- 24 large snails, prepared
  (page 174)
- 3 cloves garlic, chopped
- 6 large tomatoes, de-seeded
  and chopped
- 1 bunch basil, coarsely
  chopped
- salt and freshly ground pepper
- cooked fresh pasta, to serve

1.
Heat 3 tablespoons of the oil in a sauté pan, add the ham, snails and garlic and brown over medium heat for 3 minutes. Reduce the heat to low, add the chopped tomatoes and cook for another 45 minutes, stirring occasionally.

2.
When the snails are cooked, turn off the heat and leave to cool. Add the basil to the pan along with the remaining oil and season with salt and pepper.

3.
Serve the snails, tomato and ham with cooked fresh pasta.

NOTE
If you would like to serve this dish in the snail shells, these must be perfectly clean and dry. Boil the empty shells for 30 minutes in a saucepan of water, then leave them to dry in the sun or in a hot oven with the oven door open until completely dry.

SNAIL BROTH WITH SPINACH AND RICE VERMICELLI

Serves 4

Preparation time:
15 minutes, plus snail
    preparation

Cooking time:
1 hour 10 minutes

- 2 tablespoons olive oil
- 5 cloves garlic, finely chopped
- 1.5 litres/50 fl oz (6¼ cups) chicken stock (broth)
- 24 snails, prepared (page 174), set aside the snail shells, cleaned and dried (page 178)
- ½ bunch flat-leaf parsley, coarsely chopped
- 150 g/5 oz spinach, stalks removed and coarsely chopped
- 100 g/3½ oz rice vermicelli
- salt and freshly ground pepper
- soy sauce, to serve

1.
Heat the oil in a large flameproof casserole (Dutch oven) over low heat, add the garlic and cook for 15 minutes. Pour in the chicken stock (broth), add the snails and cook for another 45 minutes, keeping the pan over low heat all the time.

2.
Add the chopped parsley and spinach, bring to the boil and boil for 2 minutes. Turn off the heat. Immediately plunge the vermicelli into the casserole and leave to soak for 1 minute, or until softened.

3.
Serve the snail broth in large bowls. Leave each diner to add seasoning according to their personal taste, placing soy sauce, salt and pepper on the table.

HARE BOUILLON INFUSED WITH HERBS DE MAQUIS

Serves 4

Preparation time:
20 minutes

Infusing time:
10–15 minutes

Cooking time:
1 hour 10 minutes

- 2 saddles of hare, on the bone
- 4 tablespoons olive oil
- 250 ml/8 fl oz (1 cup) beef bouillon
- 4 tablespoons soy sauce
- ¼ bunch rosemary, coarsely torn
- ¼ bunch oregano, coarsely torn
- ¼ bunch wild thyme, coarsely torn
- salt and freshly ground pepper

1.
Using a very sharp knife, remove the fillets from the saddles of hare (you can ask your butcher to do this for you), then season with salt and pepper. Crush the bones using a large knife or a pair of kitchen scissors (shears).

2.
Heat 2 tablespoons of the oil in a large flameproof casserole (Dutch oven) over high heat, add the crushed bones and fry for 10 minutes until coloured all over. Pour in the beef bouillon, reduce the heat to low and simmer for 45 minutes.

3.
Strain the bouillon through a fine sieve (strainer) into a small saucepan and bring to the boil. Turn off the heat and add the soy sauce and herbs. Stir to mix, cover the pan and let infuse for 10–15 minutes.

4.
Heat the remaining oil in a frying pan or skillet over high heat, add the hare fillets and sear for 3–5 minutes on each side, or until coloured all over and cooked through.

5.
Remove the fillets from the pan and cut into thin slices. Arrange them in 4 soup plates. Pour the herb bouillon on top, season with salt and pepper and serve.

DANDELION LEAVES WITH CHORIZO AND BEAUFORT CHEESE

Serves 4

Preparation time:
25 minutes

Cooking time:
10 minutes

- 100 g/3½ oz chorizo, skin removed and cut into very thin slices
- 500 g/1 lb 2 oz dandelion leaves (greens)
- 5 tablespoons walnut oil
- 2 tablespoons sherry vinegar
- 100 g/3½ oz Beaufort cheese, cut into thin shavings

1.
Preheat the oven to 170°C/340°F/Gas Mark 3–4.

2.
Spread the chorizo slices out on a large non-stick baking sheet and dry them out in the oven for 10 minutes. Remove from the oven and leave to cool.

3.
Mix the dandelion leaves (greens) in a large bowl with the oil and vinegar. Add the chorizo slices and mix in well. Transfer the salad to a large serving platter, sprinkle over the cheese shavings and serve.

NOTE
Gather dandelion leaves before the plants are fully in flower, otherwise they will become too bitter. Dandelions tend to grow on any areas of land where there are no trees, such as meadows, fields and banks. To prepare the leaves, wash them in plenty of water, then drain them, remove the stalks and dry with a clean dish towel.

LAMB CHOPS MARINATED WITH HERBS

Serves 4

Preparation time:
15 minutes

Marinating time:
12 hours

Cooking time:
10 minutes

- 4 sprigs rosemary
- 5 sprigs wild mint
- 4 sprigs savory or thyme
- 4 sprigs oregano
- 8 thick lamb chops
- 2 cloves pink garlic, chopped
- 5 tablespoons olive oil
- salt and freshly ground pepper
- baked potatoes, to serve
- fresh herbs, to decorate

1.

The day before, put the herbs on a plate with the lamb chops and garlic. Drizzle with the oil, cover with clingfilm (plastic wrap) and leave to marinate for 12 hours in the refrigerator.

2.

The next day, drain the lamb chops and season with salt and pepper. Discard the herbs. Heat a non-stick frying pan or skillet over high heat or preheat a grill (broiler) to high, add the lamb chops and sear for 5 minutes. Turn them over and cook for another 3 minutes if you want the meat to still be pink inside, or for longer, according to personal taste. Serve immediately, with baked potatoes.

NOTE

When foraging any produce, be aware of the environment it grows in. Avoid gathering herbs and spices by the roadside because of pollution, or next to cultivated fields where crops are grown using pesticides.

NETTLE GAZPACHO WITH TOMATO BREAD

Serves 4

Preparation time:
10 minutes

Cooking time:
5 minutes

- 1 large bunch nettles (about 200 g/7 oz), stalks removed
- 1 cucumber, peeled, de-seeded and cut into small pieces
- 2 tablespoons olive oil
- 3 ice cubes
- salt and freshly ground pepper

For the tomato bread:
- 8 slices rustic bread
- 2 tablespoons olive oil
- 1 very ripe tomato, cut in half

1.
Blanch the nettle leaves for 2 minutes in a large saucepan of boiling salted water, then drain. Put the nettles into a food processor with the cucumber pieces, oil and ice cubes and process until the desired consistency is reached. Season the gazpacho with salt and pepper and set aside in a cool place.

2.
To prepare the tomato bread, preheat the grill (broiler). Arrange the bread slices on a grill (broiler) pan and toast under the grill. Brush the toasted slices with the oil and rub with the cut sides of the tomato halves.

3.
Serve the gazpacho well chilled with the slices of tomato bread.

CHEF'S ADVICE
Choose large nettle leaves to make this recipe as they will have more flavour and, most importantly, wear gloves when picking and handling nettles to avoid stings.

NOTE
The young leaves of the small, annual nettle, called *grieche* in France, are used in salads. The leaves of the large nettle, which is common and is a perennial, are cooked and made into a soup. The two varieties can also be prepared like spinach.

NUTS & BERRIES

FRESH ALMOND SAUCE WITH HERBS

Serves 4

Preparation time:
30 minutes

- 500 g/1 lb 2 oz fresh almonds, shelled (generous 1 cup)
- 1 clove pink garlic, chopped
- 25 flat-leaf parsley leaves
- 1 small bunch coriander (cilantro)
- 10 basil leaves
- 3 tablespoons olive oil
- salt and freshly ground pepper
- grilled (broiled) fish or cooked fresh pasta, to serve

1.

Put the almonds into a food processor, add the garlic and herbs and season to taste. Process, adding the oil in a thin stream, until the mixture has emulsified and the desired consistency is reached. The sauce should be smooth with small chunks.

2.

Pour the sauce into a sterilized preserving (canning) jar with an airtight lid. This sauce makes the perfect accompaniment to grilled (broiled) fish or cooked fresh pasta.

NOTE

You can keep this fresh almond sauce for up to 2 weeks, in a cool, dry place. Refrigerate once opened.

GRIDDLED WILD ASPARAGUS WITH WALNUT SAUCE

Serves 4

Preparation time:
10 minutes

Cooking time:
10 minutes

- vegetable oil, for oiling
- 600 g/1 lb 5 oz wild asparagus
- 40 g/1½ oz (scant ½ cup)
  walnut halves, chopped
- 1 bunch chives, chopped
  (optional)
- salt and freshly ground pepper

For the walnut sauce:
- 40 g/1½ oz (scant ½ cup)
  walnut pieces
- 1 tablespoon walnut oil

1.
First, make the walnut sauce. Put all the ingredients into a small food processor and process until smooth. Set aside.

2.
Lightly oil a griddle (ridged grill) pan and place over high heat. When hot, add the asparagus and chopped walnuts and sear for 1–2 minutes. Season with salt and pepper and cook for another 3 minutes.

3.
Pour in the walnut sauce and mix everything together to combine the flavours. Sprinkle with the chives, if using, and serve warm.

NOTE
The best wild asparagus is foraged in the scrublands of southern France, in Spain and the Maghreb countries of North Africa.

MY GRANDMOTHER'S WALNUT WINE

Makes 2.5 litres/85 fl oz (10½ cups)

Preparation time:
10 minutes

Macerating time:
2 months and 1 week

- 30 fresh walnuts in their green husks
- 250 ml/8 fl oz (1 cup) fruit *eau de vie* (clear fruit brandy)
- 2 litres/68 fl oz (8½ cups) red wine
- 500 g/1 lb 2 oz (packed 2¼ cups) muscovado (light brown) sugar

1.
Using a large serrated knife, cut the walnuts into quarters. Put them into a sterilized glass demijohn, add the *eau de vie*, cover and leave to macerate for 2 months.

2.
After 2 months, add the red wine and sugar, shake the demijohn so everything mixes together well and let macerate for 1 week.

3.
Strain the walnut wine through a sieve (strainer) lined with muslin (cheesecloth) and pour into sterilized bottles. Store the wine in a cool place. Drink it as an aperitif or use it for cooking.

NOTE
Traditionally, these walnuts, still in their green husks, are gathered on the French feast day of St John the Baptist, 24 June, to make this country aperitif.

WILD DUCK BREASTS WITH BLACKBERRIES

Serves 4

Preparation time:
15 minutes

Cooking time:
25 minutes

- 4 wild duck breasts, skin left on
- 1 tablespoon mixed paprika, ground cumin and ground coriander
- 2 tablespoons olive oil
- 2 tablespoons balsamic vinegar
- 250 g/9 oz (1¾ cups) blackberries
- salt and freshly ground pepper

1.
Season the duck breasts with the spice mix, salt and pepper, then score a criss-cross pattern into the skin of the duck breasts with a sharp knife.

2.
Heat the oil in a large frying pan or skillet over high heat, add the duck breasts, skin-side down, and sear for 5 minutes, then reduce the heat to low and cook for 8 minutes. Turn the duck breasts over and cook for another 3 minutes, still over low heat, basting them frequently with the cooking juices.

3.
Remove the duck breasts from the pan with a slotted spoon and put onto a plate. Cover them with aluminium foil and set aside to rest.

4.
Pour the balsamic vinegar into the pan and deglaze by scraping the cooking juices off the bottom of the pan with a wooden spoon or fish slice (spatula) and incorporate them into the vinegar. Mix in 50 ml/1¾ fl oz (scant ¼ cup) water and simmer the liquid to reduce by three-quarters. Add the blackberries and heat through for another 5 minutes.

5.
Cut the duck breasts into quite thin slices, spoon over the berry sauce and serve immediately.

DANDELION LEAF AND EGG SALAD WITH BLUEBERRY VINAIGRETTE

Preparation time:
15 minutes

Cooking time:
7 minutes

- 200 g/7 oz (1⅓ cups) blueberries
- 4 tablespoons olive oil
- 2 tablespoons red wine vinegar
- 4 very fresh eggs
- 300 g/11 oz dandelion leaves (greens), see note on page 185
- salt and freshly ground pepper

1.
Put the blueberries into a saucepan and pan-fry over high heat for 2 minutes, then tip them into a large bowl with their juices. Add the oil and vinegar and stir together, lightly crushing the fruits until combined to make a vinaigrette. Set aside.

2.
Bring a medium saucepan of water to the boil, add the eggs to the boiling water and return to the boil. Cook the eggs for exactly 5 minutes. Drain the eggs, rinse them under cold running water, then carefully peel them – the white must be set and the yolk still creamy.

3.
Arrange the dandelion leaves (greens) on a large serving platter. Cut the eggs in half, sit them on top of the salad and season with salt and pepper. Drizzle the blueberry vinaigrette over the salad and serve.

PAN-FRIED FOIE GRAS WITH BACON LARDONS AND BLUEBERRIES

Serves 4

Preparation time:
15 minutes

Cooking time:
15 minutes

- 1 × 700–800-g/1 lb 8½-oz–1¾-lb lobe foie gras, cut into 8 thick slices
- 1 thick rasher (slice) smoked streaky (standard) bacon, fat trimmed and cut into small evenly shaped lardons
- 250 g/9 oz (1⅔ cups) blueberries
- 100 ml/3½ fl oz (scant ½ cup) blueberry or grape juice
- salt and freshly ground pepper
- mixed salad or toasted brioche, to serve

1.
Heat a non-stick frying pan or skillet over very high heat, add the foie gras slices and sear for 3–4 minutes, or until coloured. Carefully turn the slices over and cook the other side for 2 minutes. Transfer the foie gras slices to a plate.

2.
Reduce the heat, drain off half the cooking fat, add the bacon lardons to the pan and fry for 5 minutes until coloured. Add the blueberries, crushing them lightly with the back of a fork, season with salt and pepper and cook, stirring, for 3 minutes. Pour in the blueberry or grape juice and simmer the liquid for 1 minute to reduce slightly.

3.
Divide the blueberries and bacon lardons among 4 serving plates and lay the foie gras slices on top. Serve with a mixed salad or toasted brioche.

DANDELION LEAF SALAD WITH CHICKEN LIVERS AND BERRY VINAIGRETTE

Serves 4

Preparation time:
15 minutes

Cooking time:
10 minutes

- 80 g/3 oz (½ cup) blackberries
- 80 g/3 oz (⅔ cup) raspberries
- 1 tablespoon red wine vinegar
- 5 tablespoons sunflower oil
- 600 g/1 lb 5 oz chicken livers, membranes removed, if necessary
- 300 g/11 oz dandelion leaves (greens), see note on page 185
- salt and freshly ground pepper
- toasted bread, to serve

1.
Coarsely crush the berries in a large bowl with a fork, adding the vinegar and 3 tablespoons of the oil, a little at a time. Season the vinaigrette with salt and pepper and stir to mix. Set aside.

2.
Heat the remaining oil in a frying pan or skillet over high heat, add the chicken livers and sear for 5 minutes until coloured and cooked. Remove the chicken livers from the pan with a slotted spoon and slice.

3.
Arrange the dandelion leaves (greens) on a large serving plate, pour over the berry vinaigrette and toss together. Place the pieces of hot chicken liver on top of the salad and serve with hot toasted bread.

VARIATION
You can also make this recipe using wild rabbit livers.

CREAM OF CHESTNUT SOUP WITH PORT AND CHICKEN

Serves 4

Preparation time:
30 minutes

Cooking time:
1 hour 20 minutes

- 50 g/2 oz (4 tablespoons) butter
- 3 tablespoons sunflower oil
- 2 plump chicken legs (preferably from a French Bresse chicken)
- 2 shallots, chopped
- 1 sprig thyme
- 300 g/11 oz chestnuts, peeled and pre-cooked
- 50 ml/1¾ fl oz (scant ¼ cup) ruby port
- 250 ml/8 fl oz (1 cup) chicken stock (broth)
- 250 ml/8 fl oz (1 cup) whipping or double (heavy) cream
- 1 bunch chives, chopped
- salt and freshly ground pepper

1.
Heat the butter and oil in a large flameproof casserole (Dutch oven) over high heat, add the chicken legs and sear for about 5 minutes, or until coloured on all sides. Add the shallots, thyme and chestnuts, season with salt and pepper and cook for 10 minutes over high heat until browned. Pour in the port and deglaze the casserole by scraping the cooking juices off the bottom of the casserole with a wooden spoon or fish slice (spatula) and incorporate them into the port. Simmer the liquid for 5 minutes to reduce by three-quarters. Reduce the heat to low, pour in the chicken stock (broth) and simmer for 35 minutes.

2.
Remove the chicken legs and some of the chestnuts from the casserole with a slotted spoon, put onto a plate and leave to cool.

3.
Pour the cream into the casserole and cook, stirring, over low heat for 20 minutes. Season with salt and pepper, then purée using a hand-held blender, until smooth and glossy.

4.
Remove the bones from the cooled chicken and coarsely chop the flesh. Cut the reserved chestnuts into pieces.

5.
Pour the cream of chestnut soup into bowls and top with the chicken meat and chopped chestnuts. Sprinkle over the chives and serve.

NOTE
If you have fresh chestnuts, prepare them following the instructions on page 30.

WILD STRAWBERRIES IN BLACKCURRANT AND WINE SYRUP

Serves 4

Preparation time:
10 minutes

Cooking time:
20 minutes

Infusing time:
2 hours

- 250 ml/8 fl oz (1 cup) red wine
- 1 tablespoon store-bought blackcurrant syrup
- 80 g/3 oz (packed ⅓ cup) muscovado (light brown) sugar
- 2 sprigs wild mint, leaves only
- 3 whole star anise
- 500 g/1 lb 2 oz (3½ cups) wild strawberries

1.
Pour the red wine and blackcurrant syrup into a saucepan and add the sugar. Bring to the boil, then reduce the heat to low and cook for 15 minutes.

2.
Pour the syrup into a serving bowl, add the mint leaves and star anise and leave to infuse in the refrigerator for 2 hours.

3.
Remove the mint from the syrup, add the wild strawberries and serve chilled.

WILD STRAWBERRY AND WHIPPED CREAM TARTLETS

Makes 4

Preparation time:
30 minutes

Cooking time:
25 minutes, plus cooling time

- 1 sheet ready-rolled shortcrust pastry (basic pie dough)
- 500 ml/17 fl oz (generous 2 cups) whipping or double (heavy) cream, well chilled
- 2 tablespoons caster (superfine) sugar
- 400 g/14 oz (2¾ cups) wild strawberries
- 2–3 sprigs mint, leaves only
- 1 tablespoon icing (confectioners') sugar (optional)

1.
Preheat the oven to 180°C/350°F/Gas Mark 4.

2.
Unroll the shortcrust pastry (basic pie dough) onto a work counter, cut out 4 circles of pastry with a pastry (cookie) cutter and use them to line 4 x 9-cm/3½-inch tartlet pans.

3.
Prick the lined pastry cases (shells) with a fork, line with baking parchment and fill with baking beans or pie weights. Bake in the oven for 15 minutes. Remove the pastry cases from the oven and remove the baking parchment and beans or weights. Return the empty pastry cases to the oven and bake for another 10 minutes. Remove from the oven and let cool.

4.
Whip the cream in a freestanding mixer or with an electric beater until it is holding its shape, gradually whisking in the caster (superfine) sugar a little at a time.

5.
Spoon a generous amount of cream into each tartlet case and arrange the wild strawberries and mint leaves attractively on top. Dust with icing (confectioners') sugar, if using, and serve.

ARBUTUS BERRY, CHERRY AND VANILLA JAM

Makes 4 x 500-ml/17-fl oz jars of jam (jelly)

Preparation time:
25 minutes

Macerating time:
12 hours

Cooking time:
10 minutes, plus cooling time

- 500 g/1 lb 2 oz arbutus berries (madrones)
- 500 g/1 lb 2 oz (3⅓ cups) pitted cherries
- 1 kg/2¼ lb (5 cups) jam (gelling) sugar
- 2 vanilla pods (beans), split in half lengthways
- juice of 3 lemons
- 200 ml/7 fl oz (scant 1 cup) apple juice

1.
The day before, rinse the arbutus berries (madrones) and remove their stalks and leaves, then put the berries into a large bowl with the cherries, sugar, vanilla pods (beans) and lemon juice and leave to macerate in the refrigerator for 12 hours.

2.
The next day, transfer the arbutus berries, cherries and vanilla pods with their macerating liquid to a large heavy saucepan or a copper preserving pan, add the apple juice and cook for about 10 minutes over low heat, stirring with a wooden spatula.

3.
Once reduced, remove the vanilla pods, pass the jam (jelly) through a vegetable mill or mouli, then carefully pour it into 4 × 500-ml/ 17-fl oz sterilized preserving (canning) jars while still hot. Seal them with tight-fitting lids and turn the jars upside down until the jam has cooled.

FIGS STUFFED WITH SPICED WILD BOAR

Serves 4

Preparation time:
35 minutes

Cooking time:
25 minutes

- 500 g/1 lb 2 oz wild boar meat, cut into pieces
- 2 cloves garlic, minced
- 5 sprigs flat-leaf parsley, chopped
- 1 tablespoon curry powder
- 1 egg
- 16 figs
- salt and freshly ground pepper
- green salad, to serve

1.
Put the wild boar meat through a mincer (grinder) and put into a large bowl. Add the garlic, parsley and curry powder. Season with salt and pepper, then add the egg and mix together with your hands until combined. Set aside.

2.
Preheat the oven to 170°C/340°F/Gas Mark 3–4.

3.
Cut a cross in the top of each fig. Open the figs out and stuff them with the wild boar mixture. Place the stuffed figs in an ovenproof dish and cook in the oven for 25 minutes.

4.
Serve the filled figs with a green salad.

NOTE
Any very strongly flavoured meat, especially game, marries particularly well with spices such as curry powder, as in this recipe. You can also use ground pepper, nutmeg, juniper berries, coriander, cumin, star anise... the choice is endless.

WILD FIG TART

Serves 6

Preparation time:
15 minutes

Cooking time:
35 minutes, plus cooling time

- 1 sheet ready-rolled all-butter puff pastry
- 2 tablespoons blackberry jam (jelly)
- 20 very ripe figs, cut into quarters
- 2 tablespoons muscovado (light brown) sugar
- vanilla ice cream, to serve

1.
Preheat the oven to 200°C/400°F/Gas Mark 6 and line a baking sheet with baking parchment.

2.
Unroll the puff pastry onto the lined baking sheet and brush with the blackberry jam, leaving a 1-cm/½-inch border. With a sharp knife, lightly score the border. Arrange the figs on top of the jam and sprinkle over the sugar. Bake in the oven for 35 minutes.

3.
Remove the tart from the oven and leave to cool. Serve with vanilla ice cream.

NOTE
Figs are a delicate fruit and cannot be stored for long. There are two main varieties of fig: white and purple. The latter are juicier and have a better flavour. Figs work particularly well with duck and rabbit.

WILD BLACKBERRY JELLY

Makes 6 x 350-g/12-oz jars of jelly

Preparation time:
25 minutes

Pressing time:
12 hours

Cooking time:
5 minutes, plus cooling time

- 1.2 kg/2½ lb (8⅓ cups) blackberries
- 750 g/1 lb 10 oz (3¾ cups) jam (gelling) sugar
- 200 g/7 oz (1½ cups) raspberries

To serve:
- toasted brioche slices or sliced rustic bread
- butter

1.

The day before, wash the blackberries thoroughly and put them into a large heavy saucepan. Pour in 100 ml/3½ fl oz (scant ½ cup) water and bring to the boil. Remove from the heat. Lift out the blackberries and set a few aside. Transfer the rest to a fruit press or jelly bag set over a large bowl. Squash the fruits to reduce them to a purée, place a weight on top and leave for about 12 hours so the juice is pressed out of the fruits – they will produce about 1 litre/34 fl oz (4¼ cups) juice.

2.

The next day, mix the blackberry juice with the sugar in a large saucepan and cook over medium heat for 5 minutes. Stir in the reserved blackberries and the raspberries.

3.

Pour the jelly into 6 x 350-ml/12-fl oz sterilized preserving (canning) jars while it is still hot. Seal them with tight-fitting lids and turn the jars upside down until the jelly has cooled.

4.

Eat the wild blackberry jelly with toasted brioche or slices of rustic bread spread with butter.

WILD BLUEBERRY MUFFINS

Makes 10

Preparation time:
20 minutes

Cooking time:
20–25 minutes, plus cooling time

- 130 g/4½ oz (1 stick plus 1 tablespoon) butter, melted and cooled, plus extra for greasing
- 100 g/2½ oz (½ cup) caster (superfine) sugar
- 280 g/10 oz (3¼ cups) plain (all-purpose) flour
- 2 teaspoons baking powder
- pinch of salt
- 2 eggs, beaten
- 200 ml/7 fl oz (scant 1 cup) milk
- 200 g/7 oz (1⅓ cups) blueberries

1.
Preheat the oven to 170°C/340°F/Gas Mark 3–4. Grease the cups of a 10-hole muffin pan with butter, unless you are using paper or silicone muffin cases (liners).

2.
In a large bowl, combine the sugar, flour, baking powder and salt. Set aside.

3.
In a second large bowl, mix the butter with the beaten eggs and milk. Add these wet ingredients to the bowl of dry ingredients and combine without over-mixing. Add the blueberries to the batter and gently fold in. Fill the muffin cups or cases three-quarters with the batter and bake in the oven for 20–25 minutes.

4.
When the muffins are cooked and a cake tester or knife inserted into the centre of a muffin comes out clean, remove from the oven and leave to cool before turning out.

FRUITS OF THE FOREST CLAFOUTIS

Serves 6

Preparation time:
20 minutes

Cooking time:
15 minutes, plus cooling time

- butter, for greasing
- 600 g/1 lb 5 oz (packed 2¾ cups) muscovado (light brown) sugar
- 10 g/¼ oz (2 teaspoons) vanilla sugar
- 4 egg yolks
- 250 ml/8 fl oz (1 cup) whipping or double (heavy) cream
- 600 g/1 lb 5 oz (about 4 cups) forest fruits (blackberries, wild strawberries, blackcurrants, blueberries)
- icing (confectioners') sugar

1.
Preheat the oven to 200°C/400°F/Gas Mark 6. Butter a small gratin dish.

2.
Mix the muscovado (light brown) sugar and vanilla sugar together in a large bowl. Add the egg yolks and whisk until the mixture is pale-coloured and fluffy. Whisk in the cream.

3.
Spread the fruits out in the prepared dish, then cover them with the cream mixture. Bake in the oven for 15 minutes until risen and golden brown.

4.
Remove the clafoutis from the oven and leave to cool. Dust with icing (confectioners') sugar and serve.

GLOSSARY

Almonds, fresh

Also known as 'spring' or 'green' almonds, they are the young fruit of the almond tree and can be eaten whole. Their thick, leathery, green coat is quite bitter and so these almonds are usually shelled and they have a delicate almond flavour. They get firmer in texture as they ripen. Young ones can be very soft – almost clear and gelatinous – whereas the slightly more mature ones have a texture similar to a soft almond.

Arbutus berries

Also known as madrone berries and strawberry-tree fruit, these berries, around the size of a strawberry, are picked from an evergreen shrub found in southern Europe, northwest parts of North America, and Canada. Red and soft, with a tartness and slightly granular texture, they are used to make fruit wines, *eau de vie* (clear fruit brandy) and a liqueur, as well as jellies and jams.

Armagnac

This grape brandy, native to the Gascony region of southwest France and produced since the fifteenth century, is generally aged for many years to develop its full-bodied, spicy aroma. Like Cognac, it is often taken as a digestif. Armagnac can be found in most supermarkets and wine and spirit (liquor) stores.

Bain-marie

A water bath formed by placing a pan, bowl or dish in a shallow pan of heated water, either in the oven or on the stove. This gentle method of heating protects delicate sauces from breaking or curdling, and allows pâtés and terrines to be cooked through evenly. A bain-marie also maintains the serving temperature of pre-cooked foods before they are dished up.

To bard

To cover a piece of meat or line a pan with strips of bacon or bacon rind, known as 'bards', to preserve moisture and prevent overcooking. The bacon melts in the heat and adds a sweet-salty flavour.

Beaufort cheese

A hard, pale cheese produced from the unpasteurized milk of cows reared in the French Alps. The young cheeses are mild and sweet, while the aged varieties acquire a stronger taste. Emmenthal, Gruyère or fontina cheeses are good substitutes if Beaufort is not available.

Black trumpet mushrooms

This common woodland mushroom is so-called because of its horn-like shape and fluted edge. Its intriguing French name – *trompette-de-la-mort*, 'trumpet of death' – is certainly evocative of its dark colour and profusion around the time of Toussaint (1 November), which is All Saints' Day in France. To preserve, thread the mushrooms on a string and hang in a cool, dry place, then simply soak them in a bowl of hot water for a few minutes prior to use. Black trumpet mushrooms impart a rich flavour to soups, stews and sauces. However, they are rare and relatively expensive, so white mushrooms or oyster mushrooms can be substituted.

Blackberries

These berries, which sprout from brambles, are small, fragrant and quite acidic. The cultivated variety, which is plumper and sweeter, grows on bushes. These juicy fruits are commonly found in jams, jellies, clafoutis and tarts.

Blanquette

This classic French dish is a ragoût made from pale meat such as veal or chicken, which is steeped in a seasoned white sauce or stock to prevent the meat from browning. Carrots, mushrooms and onions are often added.

Blueberries

Smaller and more fragrant than the cultivated blueberry, the wild blueberry must be washed thoroughly to prevent any parasites from wild animals being eaten. Bilberries, a similar fruit, grow on shrubs across the moorlands of northern and western Britain.

Bouillon

The French verb *bouillir*, 'to boil', lends its name to this seasoned broth of water simmered with beef, veal or poultry bones or vegetables.

To brown

To cook food briefly over high heat so that it turns brown, often to enhance flavour or texture.

Canner

When preserving wild foods, it is important to invest in a dedicated appliance called a canner – either a boiling-water canner or a pressure canner – which is a closed container with a lid, designed for sterilizing homemade preserves (see note, page 138). Many types are available for purchase online or in specialist stores.

Casings

A material that encloses the filling of a sausage. Natural casings are made from the intestines of animals, such as pigs and cows, whereas artificial casings are mostly made from processed collagen. Natural casings must be soaked in fresh water (20–30°C/68–86°F) before using. Soak pig casings for at least 2 hours or overnight.

Ceps

The cep (porcini) challenges the golden chanterelle for the status of most sought-after mushroom. There are more than 20 edible varieties that grow wild. Make sure, however, that the flesh is free from maggots and that it has not turned yellow, because these are signs that it has been attacked by parasites. Any damaged parts can be easily removed. Ceps are prized by connoisseurs for their earthy taste. *See* **A Note on Mushrooms** (page 239).

Chanterelle mushrooms

The chanterelle is a wood mushroom whose funnel-shaped 'cap' is adorned with pleats extending to the base of the stalk. The most highly prized variety is the golden chanterelle or girolle, which is orange-yellow in colour. It is mainly found in clumps under conifers and deciduous trees. All chanterelles have a pleasant aroma that brightens up dishes. *See* **A Note on Mushrooms** (page 239).

Chard

This leafy green vegetable, popular in French cuisine, is also known as Swiss Chard. The nutritious leaves resemble spinach, but are tougher and more resilient. The earthy stems tend to be steamed, boiled or sautéed, and can be found in vivid shades of orange and pink, as well as green.

Cross-bred duck

The result of crossing a domestic duck with a wild mallard duck. This specially bred variety is not hunted, but is readily available in France from poultry dealers. It has firm flesh with little fat and is very tasty. You can replace one cross-bred duck with two wild ducks.

Croutes

Pieces of toasted bread coated with oil or butter and commonly served with savoury toppings, such as Roast Woodcock on Tapenade Croutes (page 121) or on soups. The term also refers to bread crusts and the hardened rind of cheese. *En croute* refers to meat or fish encased in pastry, for example Fillet of Venison en Croute with Blueberry Sauce (page 40).

Curing salt mix

Curing salts are used in food preservation to prevent or slow spoilage by bacteria or fungus. Generally they are used for pickling meats as part of the process to make sausage or cured meat. Curing salts are generally a mixture of table salt and sodium nitrite. Since dry-curing sausages is done over an extended period of time, curing salts are necessary to ensure the meat remains safe, because the sausages may be eaten raw. Packages of ready-prepared curing salts can be purchased from specialist suppliers, pork butchers or chemists. More than one type of curing salt is available but for the recipes in this book it is important to buy Prague Powder #2, which is made up of salt (89.25%), sodium nitrate (4%) and sodium nitrite (6.25%). The salts work by the sodium nitrate first breaking down over time into sodium nitrite, which then breaks down to nitric oxide, keeping the meat safe to eat during the curing process and beyond.

Dandelion leaves

Commonly considered a weed, these flowers tend to grow on areas of land where trees are sparse, such as meadows, fields and banks. The iron-rich leaves (greens) should be gathered before the plants are fully in flower, because they tend to become too bitter after this stage. Roadside leaves, or those found next to cultivated fields where crops are grown using pesticides, are best avoided. To prepare the leaves, wash them thoroughly in plenty of water, drain, remove the stalks and dry in a clean dish towel. They can be crushed into a pesto paste, stirred into pasta dishes or tossed with salad leaves.

Daube

This traditional method for slow-cooking meat usually calls for cuts of beef such as chuck or blade, but wild boar or pheasant are also viable options. The meat is marinated and braised in red wine for several hours along with vegetables, herbs and seasoning. A *daubière* is the French term for an earthenware cooking pot specifically designed to retain the juices of this dish.

To deglaze

To add liquid, such as stock (broth), to a pan to loosen and dissolve brown food particles that are stuck to its bottom. These particles have lots of deep flavour and can be used to add flavour to sauces, gravies and soups.

Demijohn, glass

Also known as a carboy, this object was historically the preferred storage and transportation vessel for wine and spirit merchants. It is also used to ferment alcohol and mature wine and cider. Its narrow neck can be airlocked for this purpose, and the bottle is sometimes given handles and encased with wickerwork.

To dress a bird

Removing the feathers is a key stage in the process of preparing feathered game. The feathers are plucked from the tail upwards towards the head, and care is taken not to tear the skin. If the bird has been chilled in the refrigerator, plucking is easier. Singeing removes the remaining down, leaving the residual 'quills' that puncture beneath the skin's surface. These can be teased out with the help of a small knife or tweezers.

Eau de vie

Translating as 'water of life', this clear brandy can be made from any fruit with the exception of grapes – apricots, peaches and plums are popular options. The fruit is crushed and fermented, but tends not to be aged for too long a period in order to preserve the individual notes of the fruit. It is best served chilled as a digestif.

Fairy ring mushrooms

Most mushrooms that grow from lawns and areas of rough grass have the potential to spring up in 'fairy rings' – circular patterns dotted with mushroom heads. For this reason, the apparition of a fairy ring should not be relied upon as a determiner of whether a mushroom is edible.
See **A Note on Mushrooms** (page 239).

Feathered game

Feathered game, a category including birds hunted both in the mountains and on lowlands, includes red and grey partridge, woodcock, grouse, pheasant, and red grouse. The list of water birds includes wild duck, wild goose, mallard, teal and wigeon.

Fourme d'Ambert blue cheese

This mild blue cheese from the Auvergne region of France is produced in wheels from pasteurized cow's milk. Less piquant than Roquefort, it has a creamy, earthy taste. The blue mould appears after air has been injected into the cheese round.

Fruit press or jelly bag

A fruit press is a utensil for crushing fruits to separate the pulp from the juice. The juice is ready for instant consumption, or can be set aside and fermented to make alcohol. Traditional and modern presses are available in a range of sizes. Jelly bags perform a similar function on a smaller scale: the pulp is placed in a strainer (usually a nylon or calico bag), which is suspended on a tripod or stand over a bowl. The extracted juice is used for jellies, jams and cordials (syrups).

Girolles (*see* **Golden chanterelles**)

Gizzards

An organ found in the digestive tract of a duck or chicken, often used in French cuisine. The meat is dark, rich and flavourful, cooked in fat until tender. Duck gizzards have a crunchier texture than chicken ones, which are rubbery.

Golden chanterelles

Also known as a girolle, this highly sought-after variety of wild mushroom sprouts in clusters at the foot of woodland trees. Funnel-shaped and golden-yellow in appearance, with a slightly chewy texture, it imparts a rich nutty flavour to a host of dishes. Girolles are highly versatile and can be enjoyed sautéed in butter or matched with the strong flavours of game in stews and pies. If you are buying them dried in a package, they will require soaking before use. *See* **A Note on Mushrooms** (page 239).

Hare
Due to the gamey character of the flesh, hare might not be as widely available, or popular, as rabbit or venison. However, its rich, dark meat pairs well with the strong flavours of wine and wild herbs, and brings great depth of flavour to sauces. Jugged hare, a traditional French stew, is slow-cooked until the meat is tender.

Haunch
The back legs of a four-legged animal, such as deer, are often used for roasts. A haunch of venison makes for a richly flavoured roast. The joint is often marinated or barded before cooking to improve the tenderness of the meat.

Hedgehog mushrooms
This variety of fungi is also known as 'sweet tooth', due to the small, pointy protrusions on the lower cap. They are commonly found on the ground, but also grow on wood. In appearance, they range from pale cream to darker orange-brown shades, and their sweet, nutty flavour bears a resemblance to girolles. They work well when sautéed, fried, stewed or dried.
See **A Note on Mushrooms** (page 239).

Herbs de Maquis
The Maquis refers to the dense shrubberies blanketing more than half the island of Corsica, which lend this French province the name 'the Scented Isle'. A melange of herbs is harvested from the Maquis, including basil, mint, thyme, rosemary, oregano and cayenne. This aromatic blend is all-pervasive in Corsican cuisine, particularly seafood specialities, and imparts a delicate aroma to local oils and honey.

Jam (gelling) sugar
A type of sugar used to make jams, jellies and preserves, which contains pectin as a gelling agent. Pectin is essential to achieve the required consistency and firmness. Jam sugar has a shorter shelf life than caster (superfine) sugar because of its pectin content.

Lardons
These strips or cubes of cured pork fat, from the belly (side) of the pig, are commonly used in French cuisine to flavour savoury dishes. They add a salty depth of flavour to dishes such as Jugged Hare (page 68). Bacon sliced into matchsticks can be used as an alternative.

Mallard duck
The largest and most common wild duck in France, mallard is also prevalent in the USA and the UK. Lean with a gamey texture, it is often roasted; works well in stews; and can be potted with vegetables.

Maturation
The maturation process consists of hanging game in a cool, dry, well-ventilated place so that the flesh tenderizes and develops a distinctive flavour. While small birds are eaten as soon as they are shot, woodcock can be hung like duck, pheasant and partridge. Large game is quickly gutted (field dressed) and then hung for 1–3 days. Small, furred game is left to 'go stale' for 2–4 days.

Milk cap mushrooms
These mushrooms appear in deciduous forests in shades of orange, yellow and pink, and are named after the milky liquid that seeps from the broken flesh. They are also known as 'saffron milk caps'. Their mild taste becomes bitter after a period. They are usually eaten cut into strips and slow-cooked in casseroles and stews.
See **A Note on Mushrooms** (page 239).

Onion squash
Variously known as onion squash, red kuri squash, or orange Hokkaido, the French term for this vegetable, *potimarron*, is a portmanteau of *potiron* (pumpkin) and *marron* (chestnut). The firm flesh has a nutty character, and is perfect for baking and roasting. Whether roasted in wedges or puréed in soups, onion squash adds colour and warmth to a range of dishes.

Pain d'epices
While the recipe varies from region to region, this classic French loaf cake is generally spiced with ground cinnamon, ginger, nutmeg and cloves, and sweetened with honey. It is often sold at markets and eaten over the Christmas period. It also serves as a popular starter (appetizer) when topped with foie gras, pâté or cheese, and works well with venison. Dry gingerbread can be used as an alternative.

Pheasant

These birds are known for their lean, gamey meat. The cultivated variety, which are bred and released shortly before the hunting season, have less flavour than wild pheasant, and do not need to be hung. The meat pairs well with seasonal ingredients, including chestnuts, blueberries, squash and mushrooms. Younger pheasants are ideal for roasting whole, whereas the older birds suit pies, casseroles and stews. The sinewy legs tend to be tougher, so respond well to a slow braising process.

Partridge

The two most common types of partridge are the red-legged partridge and the grey. The rock partridge, which is highly prized gastronomically, is far more rare (see note on page 114). Partridge meat is flavoursome and tender, and benefits from the bird having been hung for a few days to develop a gamey character.

Pied bleu mushrooms

These fleshy mushrooms are distinguishable by the purplish or lilac-blue patches over all or part of their cap and stalk. After cooking, their tender flesh has a sweet flavour, which is very distinctive and fragrant. They make the ideal accompaniment to white meats or fish. See **A Note on Mushrooms** (page 239).

Pink garlic

Thought to have grown around the medieval town of Lautrec in southern France since the Middle Ages, pink garlic is the recipient of the prestigious 'Label Rouge' certification, an official mark of quality. It has a subtle taste that is sweeter and milder than the common white variety. Once harvested and dried, it can be used to flavour a wide range of dishes. Ordinary garlic can be used as an alternative.

Purslane

This edible wild plant has a high nutritional value and crunchy, lemony taste, making it a worthy addition to salads, soups or stews. It thrives in both fertile and arid soils, and can be found in many Asian and European regions in gardens, fields, wasteland and roadsides.

Quail

A small migratory bird, similar to a partridge, from the pheasant family. It is prized for its lean, delicately flavoured meat. Quails shot in the autumn (fall) months are round and plump and do not require hanging.

Rabbit, wild

This meat is pale pink, very tender and contains very little fat. It goes well with aromatic herbs and spices. Young rabbits are kept for roasting, casseroling or to be jugged, while older rabbits are made into terrines.

Ragoût

The broad term for a stew of meat, poultry or fish prepared in a seasoned sauce. Vegetables are often added to bulk out the stew and add texture. The term derives from the verb *ragoûter*, meaning 'to restore the appetite'.

Savory

Two varieties of this aromatic plant are commonly found: summer savory, with its lilac flowers and delicate hints of mint and thyme, and winter savory, distinguishable by its white flowers and more bitter flavour. Savory brings a bold, peppery taste to dishes, and works particularly well with other wild offerings, such as duck, mint and mushrooms.

Snails

Land snails appear as a delicacy on the menu in many European countries, most notably France, but also in Germany, Italy, Spain and Greece. They are also eaten in the USA. Snail foraging is regulated in some countries, either to protect against the diseases they can carry, or to preserve the population, so be sure to make enquiries about local restrictions and authorized dates before undertaking any foraging. You can gather snails in your own garden but, on the other hand, when you can do so is governed by the laws of nature. Snails are best collected at dawn or dusk, as they are nocturnal creatures. They are popularly eaten with garlic and parsley butter.

To sterilize

To sterilize jars and lids, wash them in hot soapy water, rinse, and dry in an oven preheated to 250°F /120°C/Gas Mark ½. Alternatively, put into a dishwasher and make sure they are dry before using.

Treviso raddichio

A mild variety of raddichio, Treviso is a vibrant type of chicory also known as Italian red lettuce or red chicory. It is distinguishable by its delicate crinkled leaves, magenta-purple colour and white veins. It can be served fresh or cooked, its slightly bitter flavour mellows after grilling, sautéing or roasting. Other types of chicory can be used as a substitute.

Vegetable mill or mouli
A hand-operated kitchen utensil. Vegetables are pushed against a grater, creating a much finer product suitable for purées, or any dish requiring sliced, grated or shredded vegetables. Various sizes are available.

Venison
In France, the term 'large game' includes doe (female deer of any species), ibex, red deer, chamois, roe deer, fallow deer, moufflon (a species of wild sheep) and wild boar. The term is also known collectively as 'venison' or 'black meat'. Venison is generally understood to refer to deer meat, which is championed for its rich and gamey character. In the UK, most venison comes from roe deer and red deer and is widely available in supermarkets. In the USA, venison also includes moose, elk and white-tailed deer and is available from specialist stores and online. In this book, when a recipe calls for venison, the type of deer is specified but you can substitute it with other types of deer meat.

Ventrèche
Made from the part of the pork belly (side) that has both fat and meat, it bears some resemblance to pancetta (which can be used if ventrèche is unavailable). To prepare it, the pork belly is seasoned and rolled up tightly, then it can be smoked or salted to produce difference varieties of the product. Ventrèche is highly versatile and can be used to bard meat or to provide a salty base to a range of dishes.

Vin jaune
A golden yellow wine that is only made in the mountainous Jura region of eastern France. Its uniquely complex flavour comes from a certain variety of grape and a particular wine-making process. It pairs well with strong cheeses. Dry sherry can be used as a substitute.

Walnuts, fresh
Also known as 'wet' walnuts, fresh walnuts are still in their green hulls and have not been dried. To harvest, the green hulls are removed along with the dry brown shells. The wet inner kernels have a crunchy but juicy texture and a mild, milky flavour. They work well in salads and sauces, or paired with a soft cheese.

Wild asparagus
This edible wild plant is usually foraged during Spring, and can be found in the USA and several southern European countries. It is elusive and can be difficult to spot, springing up in diverse terrains and wooded areas. To harvest, the spears should be cut or snapped off close to the ground. The stalks are crispy in texture, and work well sautéed, steamed, boiled or fried. Asparagus complements rice, wild herbs, cured meats and cheeses.

Wild boar
Also known as wild hogs or wild pigs. Wild boar meat is much leaner than commercially-raised pork, and has a richer flavour. In the UK, wild boar meat is generally imported from Europe.

Wild duck (*See also* **Mallard duck**)
This species of game is never hung; its delicious flesh is eaten fresh. Allow one bird for two people as, generally, only the thighs and breasts of a wild duck are eaten.

Wild garlic
Also called a ramson, it grows abundantly in warm, shady places such as forests and meadows but also close to streams. Young leaves (greens) have a distinct garlic flavour but are milder than garlic cloves. They work well with snails and in soups and salads.

Woodcock
The woodcock is a small migratory wading bird that is recognizable by its long beak. A rare bird, if it can be found, the woodcock is highly sought after as game, but hunting it is controlled, subject to strict quotas and selling it on the open market is forbidden. It enjoys a great gastronomic reputation.

Wood pigeon
In the southwest of France, the wild wood pigeon is prepared in the same way as a domestically bred pigeon (squab). Its flesh has more flavour and is very tender when the bird is young. It is roasted, grilled, served rare or even as a confit.

INDEX

RECURSE NOTES

—

Butter should always be salted.

—

All herbs are fresh, unless otherwise specified.

—

Individual vegetables and fruits, such as onions and apples, are assumed to be medium, unless otherwise specified.

—

Eggs are assumed to be medium (US large), unless otherwise specified.

—

Cooking times are for guidance only, as individual ovens vary. If using a fan (convection) oven, follow the manufacturer's instructions concerning oven temperatures.

—

Exercise a high level of caution when following recipes involving any potentially hazardous activity, including the use of high temperatures, open flames and when deep-frying. In particular, when deep-frying, add food carefully to avoid splashing, wear long sleeves and never leave the pan unattended.

—

Some recipes include raw or very lightly cooked eggs, meat or fish, and fermented products. These should be avoided by the elderly, infants, pregnant women, convalescents, and anyone with an impaired immune system.

—

Exercise caution when making fermented products, ensuring all equipment is spotlessly clean, and seek expert advice if in any doubt.

—

All herbs, shoots, flowers and leaves (greens) should be picked fresh from a clean source. Exercise caution when foraging for ingredients; any foraged ingredients should only be eaten if an expert has deemed them safe to eat.

When foraging for any produce, be aware of the environment it grows in. Pick berries that are high up out of reach of wild animals and avoid gathering herbs and spices by the roadside because of pollution, or next to cultivated fields where crops are grown using pesticides.

—

When no quantity is specified, for example of oils, salts and herbs used for finishing dishes, quantities are discretionary and flexible.

—

In the United States, it is illegal to sell meat from any animal that has not passed inspection by a United States Department of Agriculture (USDA) inspector. As such, it may prove difficult to buy wild game. If you are unable to hunt or shoot game yourself, or to find wild game meat at a specialty store, you can substitute the wild meat with its farm-raised equivalent.

—

When a recipe calls for venison, the type of deer is specified but you can substitute it with other types of deer meat.

—

Both metric and imperial measures are used in this book. Follow one set of measurements throughout, not a mixture, as they are not interchangeable.

—

All spoon and cup measurements are level, unless otherwise stated. 1 teaspoon = 5 ml; 1 tablespoon = 15 ml.

—

Australian standard tablespoons are 20 ml, so Australian readers are advised to use 3 teaspoons in place of 1 tablespoon when measuring small quantities.

A NOTE ON MUSHROOMS

—

The golden rules of mushroom foraging:

- Never reveal where you find your mushrooms; that must remain a well-guarded secret.
- Only gather mushrooms that you are absolutely sure are safe to eat and which have been deemed safe to eat by an expert.
- Only pick those that are young, fresh, healthy and whole.
- Do not pull up mushrooms or cut them level with the ground, but remove them gently, lifting them out with a knife.
- As soon as you have gathered them, give the mushrooms a cursory cleaning.
- Use a very large, well-ventilated basket to gather your mushrooms.

There is no point in foraging for mushrooms if the sun has been shining for 2 weeks or more because mushroom shoots always appear after a good shower. Also, don't gather them when it is raining, because they will be full of water and too spongy. It's best to search in woods that are not too dense, or on the edge of forests, where the sun can penetrate through the foliage. When you first spot a mushroom, it's tantalizing knowing that it's almost yours.

To prepare wild mushrooms, quickly rinse them in a colander under cold running water, dry with paper towels and remove the soil-covered base of the stalks. Golden chanterelles must be cleaned with a brush to remove any earth (soil) lodged in the pleats of their caps. If there is too much earth to brush away, rinse them quickly under cold running water in a colander and carefully dry the mushrooms with a clean cloth. Avoid gathering young golden chanterelles that are shaped like big office drawing (push) pins because they can be confused with poisonous mushrooms.

Phaidon Press Limited
Regent's Wharf
All Saints Street
London N1 9PA

Phaidon Press Inc.
65 Bleecker Street
New York, NY 10012
phaidon.com

First published 2016
© 2016 Phaidon Press Limited
ISBN 978 0 7148 7222 3

Recipes from the Woods: The Book of Game and Forage originates from *Retour de Chasse* by Jean-François Mallet © Larousse 2013

A CIP catalogue record for this book is available from the British Library and the Library of Congress.

Commissioning Editor: Emilia Terragni
Project Editor: Sophie Hodgkin
Production Controller: Leonie Kellman

Cover design by João Mota
Artworked by Michael Wallace
All photographs by Jean-François Mallet, except that on page 85 taken by Andy Sewell

The publisher would like to thank Theresa Bebbington, Clare Churly, Hannah Kaspar, Diana LeCore, Jean-François Richez, Ellie Smith, Kathy Steer, Wendy Sweetser and Lauren Utvich for their contributions to the book.

Printed in China